Powerful Work Hacks

THE FUTURE OF WORK

Powerful
Work Hacks

DENNIS MARK

MICHAEL DAM

Marshall Cavendish
Business

Published in 2023 by Marshall Cavendish Business
An imprint of Marshall Cavendish International

A member of the
Times Publishing Group

The publisher makes no representation or warranties with respect to the contents of this book, and specifically disclaims any implied warranties or merchantability or fitness for any particular purpose, and shall in no event be liable for any loss of profit or any other commercial damage, including but not limited to special, incidental, consequential, or other damages.

Other Marshall Cavendish Offices:
Marshall Cavendish Corporation, 800 Westchester Ave, Suite N-641, Rye Brook, NY 10573, USA • Marshall Cavendish International (Thailand) Co Ltd, 253 Asoke, 16th Floor, Sukhumvit 21 Road, Klongtoey Nua, Wattana, Bangkok 10110, Thailand • Marshall Cavendish (Malaysia) Sdn Bhd, Times Subang, Lot 46, Subang Hi-Tech Industrial Park, Batu Tiga, 40000 Shah Alam, Selangor Darul Ehsan, Malaysia

Marshall Cavendish is a registered trademark of Times Publishing Limited

National Library Board, Singapore Cataloguing in Publication Data
Name(s): Mark, Dennis. | Dam, Michael, author.
Title: Powerful work hacks / Dennis Mark, Michael Dam
Other Title(s): Future of work.
Description: Singapore : Marshall Cavendish Business, 2023.
Identifier(s): ISBN 978-981-5113-80-8 (paperback)
Subject(s): LCSH: Career development. | Vocational guidance. | Success in business.
Classification: DDC 650.1--dc23

Printed in Singapore

Contents

WELCOME TO THE FUTURE OF WORK

Remote working, automation, co-working spaces, diversity and inclusion – the workplace is undergoing unprecedented change. In order to stay not just relevant, but productive and successful, today's professionals will need to upgrade their work practices and skills.

Powerful Work Hacks presents you with highly effective "hacks" that can be put into practice right away. These tools are designed to improve personal productivity, increase job fulfilment, promote mental well-being, accelerate career growth, and ensure future-readiness.

The Future of Work is a game-changing collection of business books that explore the rapidly evolving landscape of work today. Within the next five years, many jobs will disappear, many will be created, but what is certain is that all will change. The titles in this new series, written by some of the most influential business leaders, thought leaders, practitioners and consultants in the industry, cover everything from business trends and technological innovations, to revolutions in work culture and the critical skills you'll need in order to stay ahead of the curve.

Who, What, Why

Who?
- Internal: Co-workers, other teams, manager, executives, HQ
- External: Customers, suppliers, service providers, partners

What? Money, terms & conditions, time, job assignment, other non-monetary items

Why? Strive for win-win

Good Negotiator

Analysis approach
- True issues and parameters
- Assess possible trade-offs
- Determine boundary conditions:
  - Desired outcome value
  - Walkaway value
- Best guess of other side's walkaway value

Create win-win
- Build trust
- Ask lots of questions – knowledge is power
- Create trade-offs
- More than 1 option at the same time

Tips
- Maintain professionalism
- Respect cultural differences
- Document progress and status
- Don't over-promise
- Think long-term

Common mistakes
- Wanting to win at all cost
- Win-lose assumption
- Taking information at face value
- Not considering other's perspective
- Over-confidence

Work Hacks for Negotiation

Negotiating means having a formal discussion with someone in order to reach an agreement. Even if we don't realize it, we negotiate frequently. We negotiate with people at work, our friends, family members and even strangers. We negotiate on all kinds of activities such as where to go eat, which movie to see, where to shop, what to buy, which work assignments to work on first, and how much salary is fair. Being good at negotiating is a valuable skill in any job and position in the company. The more responsibilities you have as you move to higher positions, the more critical your negotiation skills. Good negotiators get results, achieve win-win outcomes and build productive working relationships. You will find that successful employees and managers are very good negotiators.

WHAT DO NEGOTIATIONS INVOLVE?

Money comes to mind when we think about negotiations, but there are many other items we negotiate over. I'll describe some common ones here.

- **Money**. This is a popular negotiation term. When we go shopping, we may bargain over the price of an item. Buying a car is synonymous with negotiating. I remember being afraid of getting ripped off, and having to negotiate in order to not pay too much for my car at the dealership.

- **Terms and Conditions**. When we rent an apartment or buy a house, we need to come to an agreement with the other party over items in addition to money. One such item is called "Terms and Conditions" (T&C). If you are renting an apartment, the T&C to negotiate include the duration of the lease, number of people living in the apartment, early lease termination and alterations to the apartment. While the landlord may be firm on some of these items, they could be open to negotiation on other items.

- **Time.** I hire a general contractor to build an additional room to my house and I want the project to be completed in two months but the contractor has a much longer time frame in mind. A similar situation at work would be if you're starting on a project for which your boss has a deadline in mind. As you're scoping out the project schedule, you realize you need more time. Or you would like to take your vacation on a certain date and your boss is afraid that the project may not be completed. These are examples of negotiating over the time component.

- **Job assignments**. Job assignments are another item you may negotiate over. Your boss has a list of job assignments that he would like you to take on; however, you're already working on other projects and can't take on additional tasks. Or you're working on a project and the project leader is discussing with you about your deliverables. However, certain tasks on that list you don't find interesting and you would rather take on other more exciting tasks.

- **Other non-monetary items.** You can exchange one item for another, or exchange your service for something tangible or the service of another person. For example, you propose to fix a friend's car and in exchange, he agrees to build you a storage cabinet. Or in negotiating a job offer, you may want to take less pay in exchange for a more flexible work schedule. And if you represent a professional union, you may negotiate over health benefits.

As you can see, negotiating situations can occur in our professional life or personal life, at work or at home or practically any place, even online. However, for the purpose of this chapter, we'll focus on work situations. My objective here is to provide you a successful negotiation approach to any work situation.

WHOM DO YOU NEGOTIATE WITH?

- **Inside the company**. This includes anyone employed by the company such as co-workers on your team, co-workers on other teams, your manager and the executives of the company. Keep in mind that if you work for a multinational company that has business offices in other countries also, you need to be aware of cultural differences and language barriers when negotiating.

- **External party**. This includes customers, suppliers, service providers, competitors, industry partners, government agencies, etc.

WHAT IS THE GOAL OF NEGOTIATING?

The goal is to reach an agreement that is better for you than without an agreement!

- **Strive for a win-win.** Contrary to what many people believe, the purpose of negotiating is not to get the best deal for you at the expense of the other party. You may wonder why this is not a good thing. After all, doesn't it demonstrate how shrewd you are in getting the most for yourself? And if the other party wasn't smart enough to look out for themselves, well, that's not your problem. While this may give your ego a boost, it's not a successful strategy in the long run, especially in the workplace. If the other party realizes they've been had or taken advantage of by you, they likely will carry a grudge and are much less likely to negotiate with you in good faith in the future. If they do, it would be under a cloud of suspicion and mistrust, which is not a good recipe for achieving a good, professional working relationship. The ideal outcome is a mutual agreement that both parties are satisfied with. In many Asian cultures, negotiation is a way of life in certain markets and regions. Negotiation combined with "face-giving" practices forms a key part of the win-win outcome and promotes sustainable partnerships.

ANALYSIS APPROACH FOR SUCCESSFUL NEGOTIATIONS

As described in the book *Negotiating Rationally* by Max H. Bazerman and Margaret A. Neale (Neale, 1993), here are the key steps to help you conduct negotiations successfully.

1. **Understand the true issues and parameters of the negotiation**. While it might have been clear to all parties involved, people may get off track and forget what they were negotiating about as discussions drag on and nerves get fragile. When I was a project lead negotiating with an international company, BTP Inc., to produce a printing product for my company, I thought we were clear on the negotiation goal – to come to an agreement to design and manufacture a printing product for my company. The true negotiation issue was the price and the parameter was the volume of units. As the negotiation dragged on, got more intense and emotional, BTP's CEO went off on a tangent and accused my manager

of being a bully, not interested in their proposal and just toying with him. This had nothing to do with the negotiation issues. Finally we had to take a break for both sides to cool down, and when we reconvened, we reminded both my boss and the CEO what we were there to negotiate on.

I have also seen situations where both parties started negotiating on one issue, then got sidetracked and began negotiating on something else. Labour union negotiations are perfect examples of this. Without a clear understanding of the main issue and its parameters at the beginning of the negotiation, it is difficult to get both parties to focus and, as a result, the negotiation faces the risk of getting derailed.

2. **Assess where possible trade-offs exist**. While the parties may only talk about the factors they want to negotiate on, they may not realize there may be other variables they might want to consider trading off. In the example I cited above, BTP's executive was focusing on the highest price he could get for the product, even though there were other possible tradeoffs that would be worthwhile to consider. For instance, by partnering with a bigger company and a well-known brand, his company could get much more marketing exposure than he could on his own. Moreover, my company could help them with their quality process to achieve higher production yields as well as connect them to a broader community of material suppliers who could provide his company the same components to build but at a lower

cost. So don't get fixated on one variable in a negotiation and remember to consider all possible variables to trade off.

3. **Determine your desired outcome value and the walkaway value**. This helps you stay disciplined and not be swayed by your emotions or the excitement of the negotiation. Of course, these values are not carved in stone, but it should take something significant for you to change them. Usually a negotiated agreement comes somewhere between your desired outcome and your walkaway value. You must be certain about your walkaway value and willing to end the negotiation with no regrets if you cannot at least achieve it. The useful question to ask yourself is: "What do I do if I don't reach an agreement?" or "Would I be better off not having an agreement if I don't achieve my walkway outcome?" If it's not better, then you need to rethink your expected outcomes.

To determine your outcomes, especially the walkaway value, you need to understand your situation, your priorities and your tradeoffs. With our negotiation with BTP, the main variable was the price of the product and we had determined that our walkaway value was the break-even price where we would not lose money selling the product. Since we believed this product would help sell other products our company produced, we were willing to set the walkaway value at the breakeven price. At anything below this price, we would be better off walking away instead of having an agreement that would cause our company to lose money.

4. **Make your best estimate of the other side's walk-away value**. This can be difficult to predict and is an educated guess. If you have a good idea of the other side's walkaway value, you can try to validate your educated guess. If you find out that you are in the ballpark, you are more likely to succeed in reaching a negotiated agreement. Keep in mind, however, that the other side's value may change during the negotiation, depending on what information they learn or what additional tradeoffs exist. After discussing the possible tradeoffs my company could offer to BTP, including more market visibility for their brand, better production yield and lower cost from suppliers, they seemed more flexible on their pricing stand. Sensing this, we tested their possible walkaway value and were able to make an educated guess on their price.

STRATEGY FOR CREATING MUTUALLY BENEFICIAL AGREEMENTS

I'll discuss here how to put the Analysis Approach into practice and describe the best ways for achieving a win-win agreement.

1. **Build trust**. This is an important criterion for a win-win negotiation. When the other side trusts you, they are more willing to share information, more open to possible options and more willing to reach a mutually beneficial agreement. Spend lots of time getting to know them. People in general love to talk about themselves and their world. Don't rush into negotiation

right away. When you feel you have built a rapport, proceed with the negotiation. If you find them hesitant to talk, be patient. One good way to break the ice is to share with them some information about you. This usually enables them to be more comfortable and open up. Moreover, have these social talks outside of work where people tend to be more themselves in a relaxed setting.

2. **Ask lots of questions**. The goal here is to find out as much as you can. Information is power. The more you know about the other side's business – their priorities, challenges, needs, weaknesses, flexibility, etc. – the more you will be able to propose meaningful options for them to consider. While you probably won't get information directly from them, through the course of talking you may be able to infer and draw insight. Over several conversations, we learned BTP was at risk of losing a major OEM (original equipment manufacturer) and that loss would cut significantly into their company's revenue stream. With this knowledge, we believed they would be motivated to reach a deal with us and use our company as leverage with this OEM. Moreover, we learned their product profit margin had been declining due to their high component cost. All this information was valuable to us and helped us understand why they focused so much on the product price. In addition, it helped us think creatively about solutions that would help address their needs and enable our company to be profitable at the same time.

3. **Evaluate between expectations and risk preferences to create trade-offs**. All of us have different levels of tolerance for risk. If you tend to be more risk-averse, you may want to take a more "sure thing" deal while compromising on other terms. On the other hand, if you're a risk-taker, you may be willing to take a deal with less certainty of results but potential for bigger returns. Knowing the other side's expectations and risk preferences will greatly help you formulate your strategy. Again, the way to formulate an educated guess of this is by talking to them and asking lots of questions. With the BTP negotiation, we speculated that, given their company's vulnerable business situation at the time, they would be more likely to accept a low-risk deal in exchange for a lower price and better terms for my company. Given this, we came up with a few options.

4. **Make more than one offer at the same time**. This is a good practice to implement. If you offer only one option, the other side has limited options to respond. They either accept or reject your offer, or they can propose another deal. By offering more than one option, you have control over the options, all of which should benefit your company and achieve a possible win-win outcome. If you offer only one option and they reject it, you have reached an impasse. If you come back with a better option, they know your interest level and they can negotiate for an even better deal. If they counter-offer, they likely will counter with more favourable terms to them.

By offering multiple offers, the other side is under a certain pressure to choose and less likely to reject all options and propose their own counter-offer. You can even ask them to rank your options in order of preference and that will give you more insight into their thinking. We offered BTP three options: (1) Guaranteed large number of units at a low fixed price; (2) small initial unit volume with a higher price and then a lower price if we exceeded certain volume levels; and (3) a higher fixed price with no guaranteed unit volume. Moreover, all these options included our company's additional benefits to them – more marketing exposure, better production yield and lower supply chain cost. As we suspected, they chose option #1 since it guaranteed them a revenue stream. At the same time, with a lower price, our company would be able to achieve profitability.

COMMON MISTAKES IN NEGOTIATING

- Desire to win at any cost. Keep in mind that this is not a competition and you should keep an open mind and be flexible. I was involved in a bid against other competitors to acquire a company's product. Because this was an important product, I felt a strong sense to win the bidding war. As a result, the bidding price kept going higher, reaching a point of being unreasonable. In the end, one competitor apparently had an even stronger desire to win and ended up bidding a very high price to win the deal. This turned out to be an expensive purchase for their company. If my company had won the bid at that price, we would have lost money selling that product.

- Assuming your gain must come at the expense of the other party. This does not achieve a win-win outcome. In addition, it limits your creativity to find beneficial tradeoffs and explore all possible options. While it may be a short-term win for you, it's not beneficial for future working relationships.

- Taking certain information at face value. Keep in mind that the information presented by the other side can be skewed. Treat the other side's information and initial offer with some healthy skepticism. Instead, take their information and do your homework to validate and verify its accuracy.

- Not thinking about the other party's perspective. A key requirement for being a good negotiator is being able to seek information from the other side to help you better understand their situation and anticipate their offer or their response to your offer. Without having some idea of their perspective, you're operating in the dark and hoping for the best.

- Being cocky about attaining outcomes in your favour. This is a dangerous trap. Overconfidence induces complacency and inhibits thorough research and possibilities for creative solutions. Remember you are trying to get the best possible win-win outcome.

ADDITIONAL TIPS

- Maintain your professionalism. Don't get emotional or personal. Negotiation can get intense and contentious. There usually is a lot of ego and personal pride involved. You must be able to control your emotions, even when the other party is trying to provoke you through snarky remarks or put-downs. You don't have to take it lying down but you should also try not to lash back at them. Instead, channel all your energy to the issue being discussed. If you are not successful getting the negotiation back on track, maybe it's time to take a break so everyone can cool off and resume the discussion at a later time when ready.

- Understand and respect potential cultural and language differences of the other party if they are from a different country or background. Before engaging in the negotiation, take a little time to learn about their culture and how best to work with them. One of the common-sense practices is to avoid using your language's jargon or slang since they may not understand and may even see that as a lack of respect.

- Document the progress and status of negotiations in writing to avoid potential confusion or disagreements. At the beginning, document the negotiation issues and the parameters for both parties to make sure everyone has the same understanding. Document key milestones achieved or any changes to the negotiation issues. And if there are any disagreements, documenting them allows these to be brought up and resolved right away.

- Do your best to achieve a win-win agreement. This creates positive professional relationships and sets you up for productive future negotiations.

- Do not make promises you may not be able to keep. Don't agree to a deal if you need final approval from company management, even if you are very confident you have gotten a great deal. When I was a product manager in my early years of employment, I once agreed to purchase a large volume of a computer component for my company. I was very confident that my company would be able to sell and, better yet, it was at a great price from this supplier. I later informed my manager that I had agreed to this deal and just needed his signature on the contract the supplier would send over the next day. To my surprise, my manager was quite upset I had committed without clearing it with him. I then learned that this business division, as a business practice, does not commit to that kind of agreement since the risk could be high due to unforeseen factors outside the company's control.

As a result, I had to go meet with the supplier's sales manager the next day and renege on my agreement. After some tense discussions and my sincere effort to explain, the sales manager reluctantly agreed to void our agreement. Technically, I wasn't legally bound to the agreement since the contract had not been signed, but my words were good enough for him. Needless to say, I was embarrassed and lost credibility with the supplier. It took a lot of effort to rebuild my credibility with them again. It was a good lesson learned.

Value-add of saying yes

e.g. Respect from organization, seen as good team player

Balance

Own work done on time

Say No Smartly

To boss

- Be clear, willing to help
- Trade-off prioritization
- Offer alternative
- Strive for win-win (joint decision on prioritization

To co-workers

- Be clear; willing to help
- Explain why not, e.g. expertise, time
- Offer alternatives

To external parties

- Business reasons for saying no
- Offer alternatives

Work Hacks
for Saying No

Most of us have good intentions. We want to help and please people. We want to say yes to their requests and hate to say no because we don't want to disappoint them, even sometimes at our expense. We want to be a good team player. However, in work environments, requests and demands of your time have no boundaries. Many people are not aware of or sensitive to your time constraints, even though they work with you and see first-hand how busy you are. They want to satisfy a need they have and they assume you would let them know if you cannot accommodate.

Having co-workers value and respect you is important and is a key factor in your success at work. As I talk about in the chapter "Work Hacks for Promoting Yourself", showing ability to work well with people and being a good team player who provides value to the company is a big plus for you at performance reviews. Even more importantly, when promotional opportunities open up, you would be in a select group of people considered. After all, who doesn't like someone who goes out of their way to work with them and help them succeed?

However, the trick is to balance between getting your work done and helping other people. First and foremost, you must get your work done on time and do an excellent job before you can help others. If you fail at doing your job or are perceived as ignoring your work, your boss is not going to be happy. The ability to prioritize and balance between getting your work done and helping other people is important to your success. Be clear at all times about your job priorities, deliverables and deadlines. When you get an unexpected request, you are in a position to assess objectively your availability.

The ability to say no while expressing a sincere desire to help is a good skill to have. In this chapter, I'll offer ways and suggestions on how to say no smartly.

HOW TO SAY NO TO YOUR MANAGER

Throughout your job and career, you should expect unplanned requests from your manager to take on certain projects or short-term tasks. If you can accommodate and the request is important to your boss and gives you good visibility, by all means say yes. However, before you agree to take it on, make sure you understand clearly the task's objectives, expected deliverables and timeline. If you're unclear, make sure you ask for clarification. If you don't feel confident about the timeline or your ability to deliver some of the expected results, this is your opportunity to negotiate. You can negotiate to extend the deadline, reduce some of the deliverables, or ask your manager for additional resources in order to complete the task. Make sure that taking on this request will benefit you as well in some ways – whether you will get visibility with upper management, credit from your manager, or a chance to learn other skills you don't have. This is not being selfish, but achieving a win-win situation for both of you.

Sometimes, however, your manager may get a request from her boss or other executives and ask you to take it on for her. In these instances, even if the task is trivial and doesn't offer much benefit to you, you may want to take it because she's doing her boss a favour and you want to make her look good.

If you're already swamped with work and feel you can't accommodate her request without jeopardizing your own work, you should say no. You don't like to disappoint our manager. But when you need to say no, there are ways to say no and still come across as a team player. Here's how:

- Ask for details of the requests, including goals, expectations and deadlines. By listening first, you show that you care and want to know as much as you can before considering. So if you end up saying no, at least you have considered and not dismissed her request out of hand.

- Be clear that you want to help, but given all the work on your plate, you cannot do so without making changes to your priorities.

- Put the ball back in your manager's court by having her help you prioritize how important her request is relative to the tasks you currently have on your plate. Don't assume that she knows all the things you're working on. Chances are she doesn't know the full picture. Explain by giving her a full run-down of what you're working on, how much time and effort they require and how much longer they will take. Then ask your manager to prioritize her request against your tasks. If she prioritizes her request higher than some of your tasks, you can agree to take it on, but only after getting her agreement to drop or delay the other less important work. If she deems that her request is not as important as your work, then she has answered her own question and, as a result, will take back the request or consider some other ways to get it done.

Be clear that it is a zero-sum game: if something gets put on your plate, something else must come off. Don't give in. If your manager is still pushing, push back by saying: "You know I'm swamped already and if I take one more thing on, I will squeeze everything in and end up doing a half-baked job and delivering poor-quality work, which is bad for me, for my team and a bad reflection on you, and I don't think we want that to happen."

- Offer alternative ideas if possible. For example, do you know someone who is capable and may be available to help your manager? Or is this something that your boss can hire outside help for, such as contractors you may know who can do the job.

- Strive for a win-win solution. The idea is to involve your manager in coming up with a solution so you don't feel you have to make the decision on your own. This way, once a decision is reached, she will have taken some ownership in the decision. And even if the decision is no, you still are perceived as a team player and you don't have to feel bad or disappointed that you let your boss down.

After the decision is reached, write a short email message to your manager confirming the decision. This is to make sure that both of you are on the same page and to avoid any miscommunication later on. It eliminates the "I thought we decided that you would do it." If that happens, you can clarify by referring back to you email message. Managers are often busy and can be forgetful.

Let's look at an example. Your manager asks you to take on a project. You learn that it will take 25% of your time for three weeks. You ask for the details, timeline and expectations. You realize you can't take this on as your plate is full. The question here is how to say no. Let's apply the steps described above.

- "I would love to help taking this on, but I am not able to, given all the things I have on my plate. Here are the major projects I'm working on currently: task 1, 2 and 3." Describe each project briefly, focusing on expected deliverables, timeline and amount of time required. Summarize by saying: "These projects are taking 100% of my time at least for the next four weeks."

- "Can you help prioritize your project with the projects I have on my plate? Is it more important than some of the projects I'm working on?" This puts the ball in your manager's court to prioritize for you. If she confirms that this is more important, then you can suggest: "How about I take this project on and delay project xyz which has lower priority until I finish this new project?" Or after understanding all your projects and the manager decides that her request is not as important, she will withdraw her project and you have your answer. Then you could offer some alternatives, such as: "I know a couple of people who would do a good job for you and they may be available. Would you like me ask them?" Or "Maybe this is something we can outsource to some of the contractors we have used in the past."

Whatever your manager decides, it's an acceptable outcome and you come away looking good since you presented yourself as a team player.

Sometimes you're available to take on a last-minute request, but the deadline is unrealistic. Don't assume your boss knows how long it takes. She knows when she wants the results, but not necessarily what is needed to get the job done. You need to set the right expectation. It's not good if you commit but cannot deliver. If you think it will take longer but you're not certain, tell your boss that you will scope it out, see what is required and come back to her with a timeline. If you learn that it actually will take longer than she would like, explain why and support your assessment with data and solid reasons.

My boss came to me one afternoon and asked me to do a professional services analysis to see if there could be an opportunity for the company to generate more revenue by offering value-add services to customers. When I asked her for the deadline, she said her boss would like to receive it by the end of the next day. While I wasn't certain how long it would take to get the data, I had a feeling that it would take longer. I told my manager I would do a quick assessment to see what is required. I then went to an IT expert in the company to get an idea. I learned it would take about three days to get the data manually because the company did not have an automated system to extract the data. I explained this to my boss and clarified that it would take five days to complete a thorough analysis with a full written report. Although it wasn't the answer my manager wanted, she understood and was able to explain to her boss. It's better to set an expectation and beat it than over-commit and miss the deadline.

HOW TO SAY NO TO CO-WORKERS

Showing ability to work well with people and to be a good team player who provides value to the company is a big plus at your performance review and when a promotion or better job opportunity becomes available. If you could help out without compromising your work, you would earn goodwill, credibility and visibility with your colleagues and their managers. You also have chips you can cash in when you need them in the future. However, if you can't accommodate the request without compromising your own work, you need to say no. Here's how to say no smartly in such situations:

- Listen to their request and ask for details and time-line to determine if you can help. Before you say no, it's important to have a good understanding of the request to help you decide. This also helps the other person know that you listened and considered their request.

- Be clear that you want to help, but can't. If you don't have the expertise to help them, let them know. They would appreciate your honesty. If you can't because you don't have time, explain that you have so much on your plate at the moment.

- Offer alternative ideas. For example, can they wait until you finish some of your tasks so you will have more time? Do you know someone else who is capable and maybe available to help? While you're saying no, you are giving your co-worker options to consider. Even though you turn them down, you come across as a team player willing to help.

Word of caution: think carefully about accommodating other people if there are risks of compromising your work. You will not get extra credit from assisting other people if you don't do a good job with your own work. We may have a tendency to think that we can take our work home and do it later, so we say yes to our co-worker. Doing this over and over a long period of time can add more stress to you and increase the risk of getting burned out.

HOW TO SAY NO TO EXTERNAL PARTIES

If your job involves working with suppliers or partners, you probably have developed professional relationships with them over time. After many hours working together and getting to know each other, you may develop a personal connection and trust with them. This sometimes can put pressure on you to say yes because you don't want to disappoint them. Here are some suggestions to keep in mind:

- Listen to their request and ask for details and determine whether you can help. If you turn them down, at least they know you have listened and considered their request.

- Focus on the business reasons for saying no. It should be why it doesn't make business sense or it's not a win-win for both of you.

- Offer alternative ideas and solutions.

The situations described in this chapter give you an idea and approach on how to say no professionally. It's an important skill that successful people I know and have worked with possess.

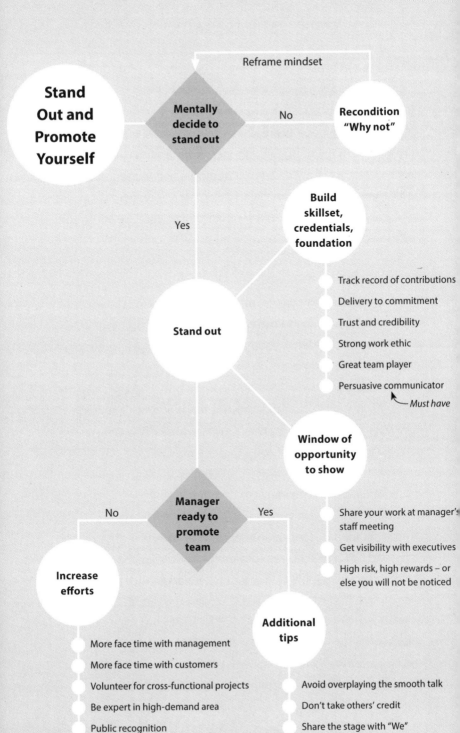

Work Hacks for Promoting Yourself

Not surprisingly, this is one of the most popular topics people asked me to write about. Many of us, whether because of our culture, the way we were raised by our parents or influenced by important people in our lives, believe that if we work hard, stay humble, don't complain and let our work results speak for themselves, we will be rewarded accordingly. This can be especially challenging in Asian cultures. Well, most of us eventually learn that we aren't going to get very far in our career with that belief. I was one of those people. From day one in my new career, I was all heads-down doing my job. I was a good worker, never complained, created trouble or bragged about my work. I also wasn't too excited about public speaking and I stayed away from speaking opportunities, especially with customers. Instead, I was happy to have my co-workers presented to the company executives and customers about our project, which I had been a key part of. And of course, my team members ended up looking good and getting the credit, at least in the executives' minds since they didn't really know of me.

I remember, to this day, about a meeting I had with my manager and her peers. When I was finished and started walking back to my office, I heard one of the managers commenting: "Michael just does his job, does what we ask him and never complains." I think they meant that as a compliment, but looking back, that didn't do justice to my career. Since they figured I was low-maintenance and not one to complain, they didn't know about my aspirations and felt little motivation to promote me when they already had people banging on their door for promotional opportunities.

Another example: After having been in the job for three years after graduating, I sat down for my annual performance review expecting a really good ranking. To my dismay and disappointment, my manager, Cindy, told me I was ranked in the middle of the pack, a mediocre ranking even though I delivered excellent results. According to her, other managers said they weren't aware of my work and the results I produced. Basically I was invisible to them and they would not agree to give me a higher ranking. It was a humbling and painful lesson for me. It taught me that I needed to take charge of my career and to make sure my work was known, valued and appreciated by not only my peers, but my manager, her peers and other executives. Over the years I got better at this as I observed and learned how other successful people conducted themselves.

With greater exposure to international media and newer international education approaches, Asians are now more open and relatively more outspoken; however, it's still a lagging factor on the international stage. For Asians working for multinational companies, you have to adapt and consciously practise standing out. While you may feel this is beyond your comfort zone, do your best to step out of it. This is critical to your career. You could be the most outspoken in the "pond" of your school, but in international companies, the competition is an "ocean".

In this chapter, we'll discuss how you can go about promoting your accomplishments, making yourself standout in the workplace while still maintaining respect and healthy working relationships with your colleagues.

- **Nail the basics**. Before you can be considered a standout performer and a star in the workplace, you must establish a strong work foundation with your peers, your manager and other executives. This strong foundation means you establish a track record of being reliable, delivering on your commitments and doing what you say you will. This must be your work ethic and not something you do once and forget. You must continue to deliver on your commitments. Continue to build on the trust and credibility with the people you work with. Once you have established and maintained your strong work ethic reputation, people will take you seriously when you want to promote yourself and management will be willing to give you more important and high-profile projects which give you more opportunities to stand out and shine.

- **Be a great team player**. Go above and beyond to help your team complete the job, deliver results and meet their commitments. Go out of your way to help your co-workers when they really need it, as long as you don't compromise your work. By doing this, you establish yourself as an important team player who puts the focus on the team and in turn, creates a positive impression in people's minds. In addition, take the time to give credit and praise to your team members when they achieve a key milestone or do something well. A simple thank you or acknowledgement message to their managers would be greatly appreciated.

- **Become a persuasive communicator and presenter**. This is a must. I have highlighted this skillset throughout this book and I cannot emphasize this enough. In order for you to promote yourself, you must be visible. How you communicate, speak and present to various audiences determines to a great extent the impression people will have of you. If you are articulate and a good presenter, people will be impressed and form a positive image of you. I have seen numerous instances where company executives were effusive in their praise about someone who delivered an outstanding presentation for the first time in front of them. This positive impression will likely be a positive factor in that employee's next performance evaluation. If you believe communication is a weakness for you, make it a priority to work on improving. Without this ability, you will face a steep uphill battle to get noticed. If you demonstrate this skill, it will go a long way to help you achieve a successful career.

- **Look for opportunities to show your work**. If your work affects other teams or provides value to them, look for opportunities to share it with them. Request time in their manager's staff meeting for you to come in to discuss and present. Although one of your objectives is to gain visibility, keep in mind that what you present or discuss must be of some interest to the audience. The topic should have a positive impact on the audience. Another idea is to use the time in the meeting to seek their input on something you and your team are working on. If some people in the audience have also been working with you, use the opportunity to give them credit and visibility in front of their manager. In the process, you are also making yourself stand out because you're the one present-ing. Make a point of doing this with different teams periodically.

- **Get face time with executives**. When you're work-ing on team projects, inevitably you and your team will be asked to review your project or give updates to company executives. When you have these oppor-tunities, jump on them, prepare and deliver the best presentation you can. These are your chances to shine. Of course, it is a high-risk and high-reward situation. However, if you hit it out of the park, you will earn great stripes and valuable credit. If you perform poorly, it can have the opposite effect. It is a risk, but if you don't take advantage of it, you will never be noticed. So embrace the opportunity, make sure you are prepared and give your best effort. Continue to look for opportunities to get in front of the executives to discuss specific ideas you have or are working on.

During my time as a Marketing Operations Director, I had a new manager after the previous manager took another position in the company. During the one year with the previous manager, I didn't meet or present to company executives at all. A month into her new job and after I reviewed my work with her, Bridgette set up a meeting for me to meet with a high-level executive team – a Senior VP, several VPs and Senior Directors – and to share with them the detailed worldwide business analysis I developed. That gave me a golden opportunity to highlight my work and get great visibility. At the same time, my new manager knew my work would be of interest to these executives who had wanted a simple way to regularly assess the company business worldwide, but had not been able to. I knew the subject matter well and I prepared thoroughly for my presentation, and as a result, my boss and I had a great meeting. The Senior VP commented that he didn't even know the company had some of the data I presented and asked to be updated on a quarterly basis. I had a manager who not only highlighted my work to her management team, but in the process, also impressed her boss and other executives.

If you don't have a manager with a keen eye for when to highlight the team, proactively work with your boss to identify opportunities to get in front of company executives. You can achieve this by showing your manager how your work is addressing a business need and would be valued by the executives.

- **Seek more face time with executives and other management teams**. Another way to get face time with executives is to ask your manager to take you to certain meetings she has with the executive team. You're not looking to present, but to be there to support your manager, to be her right-hand person. Whenever I had meetings with company executives to review progress of my team's project or to update them on an initiative, I would take one or more of my employees with me. I would introduce them to the executives, let them know that my team was doing the work and they were there to back me up. Inevitably in the meeting, there would be times I needed them to provide answers to the management team. It was a win-win for my team and me. If your manager is not intuitively looking at these opportunities, take the initiative to encourage her to do so.

- **Get face time with customers**. If your job allows opportunities to meet, present and discuss company plans or other topics with customers, take advantage of it. Customer opinion carries a lot of weight with key company stakeholders, including sales people, their management team and executives. When you meet and present to customers, the Account Sales team is usually present, and frequently company executives would be there as well. You're seen as a subject matter expert and if you come across as knowledgeable and skilful in managing customer interaction and you delivered a strong presentation, you will be sought after. Sales people aren't shy about giving feedback and if you can help them with your ability to interact and communicate with customers, they will let your manager and the company executives know. A good reputation with the sales force is one of the best ways to help you stand out. The sales teams will make sure you get the recognition you deserve. Moreover, they will seek you out for more customer engagements. While this is a good thing, you need make sure this doesn't take away the time or distract you from your core work responsibility.

When I was a product management manager, my new manager was not keen on having me travel to meet with customers. She was focused on cutting expenses and had not seen me present in front of customers to have confidence in my ability. On a customer event, we met with CIOs and IT managers to update them on the company plan and future technologies. In my presentation session, the Sales Executive team was present as well as my manager and her manager's boss – Executive VP of Enterprise Group. A short time after I wrapped up my presentation, my manager walked up to me and told me the Sales Managers were impressed with my talk and wanted to request me to come out to meet with their important customers individually. After that, she couldn't stop encouraging me to fly out to meet with more customers. Better still, the sales team's feedback was reflected positively in my next performance review.

- **Volunteer to lead an important cross-functional project**. This will enable you to demonstrate your ability to lead a team to deliver results. This may be a high-risk, high-reward opportunity and you need to have confidence in your skills and ability to successfully lead this project. Find out all you can and assess the feasibility of the project as well as your own workload before volunteering. If you want to take this project on and your plate is full, negotiate with your manager to remove some of the less important tasks from your plate.

One other idea to make a name for yourself is to look for opportunities to work directly with one of the executives on a project they need help on. For example, when I was a manager in the Product Operations group, I found out that the Senior Vice President of the Product Operations business unit needed someone to be a part-time Chief of Staff to help him manage his organization. I learned that it would take 10–20% of my time for six months. After discussing with my manager, who agreed to reduce some of my workload, I took it on and did it for a year until the Senior VP was able to hire a full-time Chief of Staff. The insights I gained on how a high-level executive worked with his team and other executives on decision-making process as well as how he dealt with organizational challenges and company politics was invaluable. In addition, I had great exposure and developed good relationships with people across organizations and those relationships paid dividends later on.

- **Be an expert in a high-demand area**. Many
  respected people who stand out in their company
  are also recognized for their expertise in a particular
  area. They could be recognized as an expert in a new
  and emerging technology, a master presenter or a
  business analyst guru, while someone else could be
  recognized as a creative marketing expert. These
  are the "go to" people who other people reach out
  for assistance. These are the people company executives assign important work. When I was in Product
  Operations, we had a person who was responsible for
  Business Analytics and Metrics. She was the person
  our manager and other executives went to when they
  needed a quick turnaround business report, a deep
  dive analysis on a business problem, or analysis to
  prepare them for upcoming meetings with industry
  analysts.

  Typically in your department, organization or company, there are "gaps" in one or more areas due to
  lack of people with the right skills, expertise or people
  with already too much work on their plate. By talking
  to your manager and other managers to find out what
  important areas are not being covered or, if they had
  the means, where they would invest the resources, is
  an excellent way to identify areas where you can take
  the initiative. Managers frequently are forced to focus
  on short-term goals that leave them with little time
  for longer-term priorities, such as what the company
  needs in the future in order to continue to compete
  successfully.

In addition, in your research, you may discover an innovative idea that will help improve your company's business. If you do, develop a proposal and discuss it with management. If they find it compelling and believe it would contribute significantly to the business, they may agree to fund the initiative and appoint you to lead it. One of the customer support engineers on my team came up with an idea to improve customer experience by reducing the time required to set up a networking system. Kent discussed it with me and I set up a meeting for him to pitch the plan to our Senior VP. The pitch went well and Kent got the approval and funding to implement a pilot. After the plan was proven to be successful, he was put in charge of implementing it throughout the company.

- **Public recognition and reward**. Most companies on a regular basis choose employees to recognize for their outstanding work, such as excellent customer service, going above and beyond, innovation, teamwork, etc. Employees are nominated by their peers or their managers. This is an effective and public way to receive recognition and a potent way to promote yourself by letting others promote you. When you have one-on-one meetings with your manager, find out what you can do to be considered for this kind of recognition. And if you have done something worthy of the recognition, discuss whether it merits consideration.

ADDITIONAL TIPS

- Self-promotion is only meaningful if you have tangible, positive work results to show. Otherwise, you come across as an empty suit. It's true that we'll sometimes see people who have gotten by with self-promoting without having meaningful accomplishments because they were excellent smooth talkers. However, this tends to catch up to them eventually when they are exposed for who they really are.

- Don't take credit for other people's work. There is no faster way to lose credibility and people's trust. You may get away with it once, but good luck getting other people to work or collaborate with you in the future. It's reasonable and legitimate to get credit as part of the team. If you're the team leader, a good way to earn credibility and respect with your team is to give credit to the entire team and then recognize key team members for their unique contributions.

- As part of a team, learn to say "we" instead of "I" as much as appropriate. Say: "We got creative and found ways to finish our project ahead of schedule" instead of "I was the one with the creative idea..." I learned this lesson early on in my career when in one presentation to update the executive staff on a team project, I apparently used "I" too many times without realizing it. A manager from another department approached me after the meeting and told me that it was a team effort and I should try to remember to say "we" and give the team credit as appropriate in the future. I realized I was being selfish without doing it intentionally. I apologized to him and explained that it was not my intention and I would learn from it going forward.

How to Manage Up

Mindset reframe
- Not butt-kissing
- Build successful working relationship with superiors
- Life skill to improve career opportunities

Complement your manager's weakness

Help your manager work effectively

Invite your manager to important meetings

Promote Yourself
→ Pg 34

Make your manager look good

Improving your position
- Be in most ready position for next promotion opportunity
- Get a management mentor
- Become a needed expertise
- Act professionally, with respect and confidence to advocate views
- Seek personal face time with key executives

Work Hacks for Managing Up

Some people view "managing up" with disdain, equating it to butt-kissing and playing politics. They hold low opinions of people who manage up well because, in their mind, these people don't really produce results and brown-nosing is the only way to climb the corporate ladder. This is certainly the case in many Asian regions where managing up is seen as bad behaviour, unproductive sucking-up. If you hold this negative view, I want to persuade you to see it in a more positive light, as an effective method to get work done successfully and help make yourself stand out at the same time. By the end of this chapter, I hope to have convinced you that shifting your mindset to balance negative views with positive ones of managing up is the right way forward. And the sooner you start, the better.

What does it mean to "manage up"? One common definition is to build a successful working relationship with a superior or manager. I would describe managing up as working to help your management be successful and for them to help you do your job effectively. Most people confine managing up to only their manager, but I think this is too narrow. Managing up includes having a good working relationship with other managers as well as executives. In order to be promoted, you need to show you already know how to work with management, how to communicate with them and how to handle yourself in their company. It's another skillset to learn and have in your bag.

Moreover, it's a skill you can apply throughout your career as you interact with executives from different companies, or in the future if you decide to go out on your own, to interact with high-power clients. It's a skill you can learn, practise and continue to improve on. In this chapter, I will discuss effective and practical ways to manage up from any position you hold in the company. In addition to reading this chapter, I encourage you to read the "Work Hacks for Promoting Yourself" chapter as it contains complementary information to what we will be discussing here.

Follow these best practices to manage up:

- **Help your manager work effectively and efficiently**. By understanding your manager's management style, you can help her be effective and successful by adapting to her management style. Managers seem to not have enough time, and they would appreciate your proactive effort to work with them. In your initial meetings with your manager, discuss how she prefers to work with you – getting updates, her hot buttons, one-on-one and team meeting structure, annual plans, etc. By proactively doing this early on, you create an environment for your manager and you to work efficiently together and reduce wasted time by eliminating guesswork and miscommunication.

- **Complement your manager's weaknesses**. Like all of us, every manager has weaknesses. For example, some managers are disorganized, some don't have good analytical skills, and some aren't good at creating compelling presentation slides, while others are not good with details. If you can discover your manager's weakness and have the skills to complement it, you will become valuable to her.

Let me give a couple of examples. I had a manager who wasn't great at and didn't want to deal with the detailed, nitty-gritty part of managing the department budget. I was good with numbers and ended up taking over this responsibility for him. It relieved him of a burden he didn't enjoy doing, and at the same time, I earned his trust and confidence by having the skills to handle the budget for him. Being disorganized was another manager's weakness. She wasn't good at organizing, following up on meeting details, and had a hard time keeping tabs of her action items. Recognizing this, one of my colleagues, who had great organization skills, volunteered to help her. Kim helped the manager come up with meeting agendas, arranged all the logistics for our department meetings, kept track of the action items from our staff meetings, her manager's meetings, and organized employee ranking sessions. This relieved her manager from having to do something she was not suited for, and Kim became her right-hand person.

- **Make your manager look good**. One of the best ways for a person to stand out is to let others sing their praises for them. Look for opportunities to do this for your boss, but make sure you do it when warranted and not just shamelessly sucking up to her. During one meeting with the US and international marketing regions to discuss an upcoming product launch, I presented the marketing plan to several Vice Presidents of Sales and Marketing. I pointed out to the audience that my manager was instrumental in helping to create a successful plan and working extremely hard with the CEO executive staff to secure a significant amount of funding for each international region. The international VPs were immensely impressed with the plan and effusive in their praise and appreciation. The Senior VP of marketing was at the meeting and heard directly from these sales VPs. My boss looked good to a very high-level executive and to other executives who would be influential when it came time for her promotional consideration. She earned the praise she received and in turn appreciated my effort to give her the credit she deserved. At the same time, I also gained her confidence and loyalty.

- **Invite your manager to important meetings**. Invite your manager to meetings where you believe she would receive useful information and be able to use it to help her with a key project she has been working on. At the same time, you may be able to gain her support for what you're working on. You may think managers have visibility and know about all the important meetings to attend; however, keep in mind that your manager can't possibly know about all the meetings you and the team have, not to mention which ones to attend. When I was working on a proposal to get money to build a number of product prototypes to promote and train our resellers, I realized that it might be an uphill battle since we had a tight budget and the company was looking for ways to cut expenses. I invited my manager to a meeting with the reseller representatives to discuss their needs for a successful channel programme. In this meeting, she heard directly from these representatives why they needed the prototypes and how the programme would help them sell the product successfully. In addition, they provided her with insight into other important business aspects, which she could incorporate into an overall channel business strategy she had been working on for the company. Walking out of the meeting, she thanked me for inviting her and appreciated the insight she received from the group. It was a win for me as well since it helped me get the funding I needed.

- **Get a mentor who can be your champion**. This should be a must requirement on your career development checklist. A mentor who is a member of the management team can provide you honest advice on how to manage up, interact with other executives, respond to different situations as well as give you visibility to a broader group of company executives.

When I first met with my mentor, a Vice President in another function my boss suggested to me, I told him that I didn't really know what managing up meant or how to do it. Through talking with him regularly, observing his interactions with people and practising what he suggested, I came to understand managing up better and more importantly, how to do it effectively.

- **Become a needed expert**. One of the great ways to manage up is to become an expert in an area that adds value to the company and helps other people do their job better. This will put you in a high-demand position and provide you with valuable opportunities to interact with the management team. When you're able to offer help to the executives, they're more likely to become advocates for your ideas and have your back when you need it.

But how do you become a valuable resource if the executives don't know you? The answer is to find opportunities to show your work and demonstrate how it can help them. When I started my new job as a Pricing Strategist, I developed a regular business dashboard for the product management teams to use. The dashboard showed company business results, trends and potential challenges. I explained to my boss how this dashboard would enable her and other managers to make more informed business decisions by providing real-time analytics and insight. She bought into it and invited me to present at her manager's staff meeting. The management team loved it and they wanted the dashboard to become the standard reporting tool.

After that I was known as a Business Metrics expert. Over time, several executives came and asked me for help with their business problems, and as a result, I gained a lot of experience working with them and earning their support. I remember distinctly a meeting when a colleague and I were to present a new initiative to a group of managers. I was nervous walking into the room because I knew several high-level managers would be in attendance and I only knew one of them, Richard, a Senior VP of Customer Solutions whom I had worked with on a business issue a year ago. At the start of the meeting, each of us introduced ourselves, and when my turn came up, Richard piped up and told everyone in the room that I was an expert at analyzing business problems and that I was the go-to person for anyone with a business challenge. Needless to say, the rest of the meeting went very well and we had full support for our proposal. Although I felt we had a strong proposal, having Richard's support helped greatly.

- **Act professionally**. In your interactions with your manager and other executives, respect their status and give them the reverence their position deserves. At the same time, don't feel that you're in a subservient position where you need to do everything they ask or agree with everything they say. You need to have the confidence to push back, to advocate your views or ideas in a polite and respectful way. Be professional and never get personal. In a meeting with a group of managers, maintain your poise and don't get rattled when they question you. The impression that people form of you is mostly optics – how you come across in your expression, your behaviour and what you say. For example, if you disagree with a manager's conclusion in the meeting, push back with something like: "I understand and appreciate your point. However, based on the information I have, I have a different view on it. Could I share my view?" Then go ahead and explain. Remember to back up your response with facts and solid data, as appropriate.

- **Seek personal face time with key executives**.
  When you have one-on-one time with your manager or other managers, they can be more themselves, and more comfortable revealing the side that you may not have seen before, and you may get a better understanding of them as people. These kinds of insight are helpful as you learn how to work with them effectively. It's difficult to get this kind of interaction but seek out opportunities. As a young Product Manager, I sometimes met with the General Manager and his staff to present recommendations on business issues such as the forecast for our products. During one meeting, the GM felt the forecast was too high and should be reduced. After

I explained my rationale to him, he still was not quite sure about my forecast. I then jokingly suggested a bet – the one who lost would buy the other dinner. To my surprise, he accepted. Well, I was lucky enough to end up winning the bet. He took me out to dinner and I had two hours of his time to myself. I learned a few important and interesting nuggets about how his mind worked, how he worked with his staff and managed up to his superior. At the risk of overstaying my welcome, I suggested having dinner periodically if he was available. To my surprise, he agreed and we had dinner 2 to 3 times a year for a couple of years.

Seek out a couple of key executives that you would like to have a one-on-one lunch with and send them a request. It makes it a bit easier if you already have a rapport with them through meetings that you attended or presented. They may surprise you and accept your invitation. After all, some executives want to keep their finger on the pulse of the company and would welcome opportunities to hear from employees. Other executives, from time to time, have open invitations where you can sign up to have lunch and discuss company business.

- **Manage up to a promotion**. Hopefully, your managing up effort to earn the management's support will pay dividends for you in the future. By demonstrating your contributions to the company, helping the management team succeed and making yourself stand out in a professional way, you put yourself in a position to be considered seriously for promotions when the opportunity arises.

Work Hacks for Performance Reviews

Employee performance reviews play an important role in our career. How we are evaluated determines to a great extent our salary increases and our chances of promotion. Beside tangible rewards, getting an excellent job review is a major boost to our confidence and standing among our peers, although I would argue that we shouldn't let our self-confidence be affected by external factors we don't have complete control over. In this chapter, I will describe a couple of employee evaluation methods being used, how you can help prepare your manager to evaluate you fairly and how to respond to your manager when you receive your performance review.

PERFORMANCE RANKING AND EVALUATION PROCESS

Companies may differ somewhat on the method they use to rank or evaluate their employees. Typically, formal job performance evaluation is done once a year. Regardless of the methodology

Performance Review

Ranking approaches
- Forced ranking distribution
- Individual absolute performance score
- Individual value and impact to organization – no performance score

Discussion frequency
- Periodic
- Ongoing year-long

Help prepare your manager
- Keep track record of results and feedback
- Share and discuss with manager regularly
- Provide list of people who know your work
  - One month prior
- Summarize accomplishments, including examples of going beyond call of duty
- Establish visibility to broader management

Handling different outcomes
- As good as or better than anticipated
- Lower rating then you deserved
- Very low rating
  → Performance Improvement Plan

Output
- **Pay increment factor**
- **Career planning**
  - Promotion potential
  - Development plan
- **Next year plan**
  - Scope
  - Above and beyond
  - Clear and realistic targets

a company uses, employees are evaluated on two dimensions – what results they achieved and how they were achieved (the "what's" and the "how's"). The former are tangible, measurable results while the latter is based on the employee's effectiveness in working with other people to produce results. The feedback from peers, partners and other managers plays a key role in how the employees are ranked or evaluated.

There are companies who are going toward the concept of managers having year-round continuous conversations with their employees and with no specific rating scores. The goal here is to avoid demotivating factors in the communication with employees and have the discussion focus on coaching and development. However, pay/reward administration is still aligned to specific individual performance factors, such as results versus goals and objectives.

I'll describe two employee performance evaluation methods many companies employ: forced ranking and individual performance review.

- **Forced ranking**. Employees are ranked on their job performance for the past year relative to other employees in similar job junctions. These companies adhere to a predetermined ranking distribution known as the bell curve. Employees in similar job functions within a department are rated relative to each other. Each department is required to adhere to the bell curve distribution policy.

  Take one of my former companies, for example. This

company ranks employees on a scale from 1 to 5, with 1 being the highest rank and 5 the lowest. Approximately up to 25% of employees can be ranked with a 1 or 2 ranking, 50% with a 3 ranking, and 25% with a 4 or 5 ranking. Employees with high rankings receive bigger salary raises and other financial incentives, including stock shares. Lowest-ranked employees would be put on performance improvement probation and likely receive no raise or other financial rewards.

- **Individual performance review**. Unlike forced ranking, each employee is evaluated individually and there is no ranking scale. Each employee is evaluated based on their performance compared to expected results described in the employee annual plan and based on feedback from the key people they worked with in the past year. Each employee's results are compared to their annual plan to determine whether they met, exceeded or did not meet expectations. The managers have more flexibility to apply salary increases based on their evaluation of the employee.

HOW MANAGERS CONDUCT EMPLOYEE RANKINGS AND EVALUATIONS

- **Forced ranking**. Prior to the department ranking meeting, the manager should gather all relevant information on each employee on his team so he will be prepared to represent his team fairly in the ranking meeting. He compiles the results for each employee relative to the goals outlined in the employee's annual plan. In addition, he gathers feedback from people whom the employees worked closely with in the past year, including team members, co-workers, partners and managers from other functions. While all managers should follow this preparation practice, not all do. Some are more prepared than others. Needless to say, managers who are better prepared stand a much better chance to get a fair ranking for their employees.

I'll describe one ranking scenario in an organization I worked in. At the beginning of the meeting, all managers give their ranking recommendation for each of their employees. Once this is done, each manager explains his ranking recommendation by summarizing the employee's results, the manager's own assessment and other people's feedback on the employee. A discussion follows among the managers in the room on whether they agree with the manager's recommendation. Based on this discussion, the employee's ranking may get moved up, down or stay unchanged. Other managers' impression of you can have a big impact on your ranking. For managers who did not have frequent interaction with you, their limited opinion may skew their overall assessment of you. While this may seem unfair, it's the reality and I have seen examples of it.

When all the managers are done with the discussions, the revised rankings are compared against the bell curve policy and if the rankings are off, adjustments will need to be made. The variance normally happens at the top ranking and at the bottom ranking band. This is where tradeoffs and compromises are made. A manager may have to give up one of the high rankings to save an employee from being included in the lowest rank band unfairly. Employees who are not known or who are perceived negatively by other managers stand the greatest chance of being moved to a lower ranking band. This can be a painful and unfair part of the forced ranking distribution policy.

Once the rankings are finalized, each manager administers his employees' salary increase and other financial rewards based on their ranking and the company's guidelines. Finally, the manager completes a performance review report and reviews with each of the employees. This report also includes next year's plan.

I want to emphasize a point here regarding other managers' opinion of you. If their assessment of you is not fair or inaccurate, the way for your manager to counter it is to be thoroughly prepared with facts and feedback on their employees from others. This is where you can help your manager.

- **Individual performance review**. This process is much simpler and less controversial. Your manager is the only person evaluating you. He compares your results to the objectives described in your annual plan; this is the "what" part of the review. He also assesses how effectively you worked with other people to achieve the results; this is the "how" part of the review. He reviews the feedback on you from people you worked with over the past year. In assessing both the "what's" and the "how's" of your performance, your manager determines if you have exceeded, met or failed to meet expectations.

HOW YOUR SALARY INCREASE IS DETERMINED

Several factors go into salary increase considerations. First is the company's business performance. If the company is doing well, employees may get better raises. If not, employees may not get any raises at all. The second factor is the result of your performance evaluation – if the result is good, you'll typically get a bigger raise. The third factor is where your base salary is within the salary range of your job level. Per your company's salary structure, each job level has a salary range, and the salary for employees with this job level must stay within this range. If you are near the top of the salary range, you may not get much of a raise even if you received a good performance review. The best way to get a significant raise is to get promoted to the next job level.

HOW TO HELP PREPARE YOUR MANAGER FOR YOUR EVALUATION

While we all want to have an excellent review or a high rating, that should not be your goal. Your goal is to get as fair a ranking or performance review as possible. One more important point: you must take ownership of helping and preparing your manager and not assume he has what he needs. I learned this the hard way. As a product manager for a computer system company early in my career, I thought that if I put my head down and focused on giving my best effort, my manager would take care of me and reward me appropriately. I was managing a several-hundred-million-dollar server business, responsible for several aspects of the business, including working with engineering to enhance the products, providing forecast for manufacturing, setting pricing and solving customers' business issues. The product line business was successful and generating better-than-expected sales and profit. I was certain I would receive a high ranking.

I looked forward excitedly to the day of my annual performance review. When I sat down with my manager, Mary, she was very complimentary on my work and results. I was feeling good. However, my excitement came crashing down when she told me I was ranked a 3 (an average ranking on a scale of 1-5). In my dismay and anger, I asked her to explain. She told me she had wanted to give me a higher ranking, but other managers in the meeting told her they didn't have visibility of my work and my contributions to the company. She told me she had tried to fight for me but didn't have enough evidence to support her argument. In my anger, I thought about leaving the company. After all, I had busted my butt, worked days, nights and weekends to help the company succeed and my reward was a lousy 3 ranking – a ranking attributed to an average performer.

I took a few days off from work. The break gave me time to think, and after I calmed down, I realized I had no one to blame but myself. I had completely and blindly relied on my manager to know what I was doing and as importantly, to let other managers know my results and contributions. Although she didn't ask me, I did nothing to prepare her. I learned a hard lesson – I had to take ownership of my career and not rely on anyone else. Even though I didn't have direct control over my job performance ranking, I had to make sure to help my manager be as prepared as possible and not assume she had it under control. In addition, I needed to make sure that other managers and key stakeholders had visibility of my work and my results. Refer to the chapter "Work Hacks for Promoting Yourself" for details.

Here are the steps to help prepare your manager to evaluate your performance:

- Keep an ongoing track record of your results and feedback as the year progresses. Don't wait until the last minute. This is too important to wait until just before the evaluation time to start writing down your accomplishments and other people's feedback. And in the rush, you may forget to include some key milestones as well as gathering feedback from all appropriate people.

- Review regularly your results relative to your employee plan's objectives. If and when your plan is revised due to changes at work, make sure you and your manager are on the same page, especially regarding the expected results. Be proactive and review this plan and your progress with your manager at least once a quarter. This is also an opportunity to capture and revise any changes in your plan if necessary. In addition, if you have been doing a good job on an important assignment that was not part of your plan, make sure you capture this accomplishment as "exceeding or going above and beyond your responsibilities" when you review your plan.

- Whenever you receive a positive message from one of your colleagues, managers, partners or customers regarding a job well done, let your manager know and keep a record. In addition, make a habit to seek out your peers and other managers for feedback on key projects you are working with them on. If they do want to give you feedback, they will appreciate your being proactive. Moreover, you get real-time feedback from them on things you can work to improve instead of hearing about it from your manager at your performance review meeting. And when it comes time for them to give feedback to your manager, they'll more likely give positive feedback on you.

- About a month before your ranking or evaluation meeting, give your manager a list of names of the people you want your manager to obtain feedback from. He may ask you for this list, but will appreciate if you took the initiative to provide him the list. These are people who can give your manager constructive feedback with specific examples from their time spent working with you. They include peers who worked closely with you on different projects and other managers who have seen your work and observed your teamwork skills.

• Provide your manager a list of your accomplishments since the last ranking or evaluation session or since you joined the company if you're new. Make sure to highlight the results compared to your annual plan – how the results impacted company business, whether the results met or exceeded the goals and/or timeline. In addition, if you took on additional important projects that were not originally in your plan, be sure to highlight this as "going beyond the call of duty" accomplishments. Among the criteria for getting a high ranking or excellent review is that you not only meet your job expectations, but exceed them. When you provide your manager the list, sit down and go over this list in person with him to make sure there is no confusion. Don't assume he will understand or remember. By going over it with him in person, you eliminate the risk of your manager reviewing your list at the last minute and having no opportunity to clarify any detail with you first.

• Take advantage of opportunities to get visibility with other executives. How other managers and executives perceive you has a significant impact on your review outcome. Look for opportunities to present in front of them and when you do, be prepared to give your best effort and make the most positive impression you can. I had one employee, Mike, who was very good at this. He would seek out opportunities to go into an executive's staff meeting to present his work or a team project important to the company. He not only gained visibility but also developed a reputation as an excellent presenter and a team leader. When I met with my boss to review Mike's performance later in the year, my boss not only agreed with my proposed high ranking for him but also wanted to give him even more raise and stock options than I had recommended.

HOW TO DISCUSS YOUR PERFORMANCE REVIEW WITH YOUR MANAGER

You have done your best and given your manager all the ammunition he needs for your performance evaluation. Now the day comes for you to have your performance review with him. Once the ranking or evaluation result is final, it's very difficult to change. I have seen only very rare cases where a ranking was changed as a result of employee escalation. Here are suggestions on how to handle different evaluation outcomes in your review meeting.

- You received a lower evaluation result than you deserved.

▷ Maintain your professionalism. If you didn't get a fair ranking you anticipated, it's certainly understandable to feel disappointed and express it to your manager. While it may be difficult, be as professional as you can and resist throwing a tantrum or making comments you may regret later. But clearly express your disappointment. Take a break if you need to calm down.

▷ Focus on the two evaluation dimensions I discussed at the beginning of this chapter (the "what's" and the "how's"). Ask him to compare your results versus expectations in your annual plan. You want him to explain and give specific examples to clarify your evaluation results. You want to probe to understand (1) if your manager prepared himself adequately with the details you provided, (2) the specific reasons you fell short in not earning a higher evaluation result, and (3) what you could have done differently to achieve a better outcome.

▷ To find out if he was prepared, ask questions such as: "Give me suggestions on how I could have helped you better prepare for your management evaluation meeting" and "Of the materials I provided you, what was most helpful and what else did you need that I didn't provide?" To probe for more specific details, ask: "I would like examples in my job performance that held me back in my evaluation", "Please give me examples of what, if I had done differently, would have enabled me to get a better outcome" or "Give me an example of where someone was able to get a better review than I was." If he makes comments regarding not working well with others, say: "Please give me specific examples where I wasn't effective working with people to get things done" or "Give me examples where other managers had a negative impression of me." Conclude this discussion with a question on what else you need to improve going forward in order to achieve a better evaluation outcome next time.

- If you received a very low ranking or very negative review, your manager probably has begun working work with HR to develop a "Performance Improvement Plan" for you. This plan spells out specific tasks with expected results and deadlines you must meet. If you don't meet them in a given period, you manager will proceed to terminate your employment. Ask your manager to provide an objective assessment of your results versus expectations in your annual plan. Focus on the two evaluation dimensions I discussed above (the "what's" and the "how's"). If you have been taking the steps to monitor your own performance and how others perceive you, you should not be surprised with the evaluation outcome. You can avoid getting into this predicament by paying attention to your manager's feedback in one-on-one meetings and proactively seeking other people's feedback. You then can take actions to improve your situation or consider other job options. By the time you hear this in your performance review, it may be too late.

Note: If you feel strongly and objectively your evaluation result was unfair and unjust, you can escalate your dispute to HR and your manager's boss. Ask for a meeting where you can objectively lay out the facts to justify a better evaluation result. As I said earlier, you would face a steep hurdle to have this changed, especially if the company uses the "Forced Ranking" process. My advice on handling this dispute is to be professional and use all the facts you have to make your case.

• If you received an outcome you anticipated or even better than you had hoped, use this opportunity to find out what you did right in your manager's views and where you can continue to improve. Ask questions such as: "Can you give me examples of what you and other people see as my strongest areas?" and "Where can I continue to improve going forward?" You may also want to have a discussion on promotional opportunities. Ask questions on what the next steps are and what you need to do in order to merit promotional considerations. Look for concrete examples and suggestions.

• The next step in this meeting is for the manager to review with you your plan for the next year. The plan should include goals, deadlines and expected results from your responsibilities and the projects you will be working on. Ask for clarification on anything you aren't clear on and assess how achievable the plan is. What parts of the plan are within the scope of your job and what parts are "going above and beyond", where if you accomplish them, they would be a plus for your next performance evaluation. Most of all, once you have your questions answered and are clear on expectations, don't commit right away, ask for time to think about it. Even just for a day or so. You have a chance to step back, clear your head and assess more objectively. Ask yourself if this plan is realistic to complete as required. Keep in mind the importance of meeting your commitments. Not meeting your commitments will affect your review negatively. If the plan is not realistic, negotiate to reduce the plan's expectations, or change some parts of the plan from "Must" to "Want" deliverables.

- Some companies' annual employee plan also includes an employee development plan. This plan is intended to help employees continue to develop skills and grow in their career. Think about what you would like the next step in your career to be and draft a plan to support that. It may include trainings or classes you would like to take, or an assignment to participate in a company-wide initiative that would give you additional skills and knowledge. Or it could be to identify a mentor who can coach and help you in your career path.

One word of advice: many managers tend to pay lip service to the development plan and don't put in a lot of effort. Managers are not really evaluated or measured on this responsibility. You should own and drive your development plan for your own success.

Effective Time Management

Prioritize
- Prioritize "To Do" list
- "Urgent vs Important" 2x2
- "Do It Now" 2x2

Reduce unproductive activities
- Block 2 hours "Priority" time
- Learn to say no
- Discipline in attending necessary meetings only
- Align upfront for presentations
- Hide from desk interruptions
- Limit breaks
- Resist browsing
- Organize emails
- Stay healthy to minimize sick days
- Work from home

Avoid time-wasters
- Social media, cell phone, texting
- Gossip, socializing
- Internet browsing
- Excessive meetings
- Emailing
- Extra tea/smoke breaks
- Interruptions at desk
- Commute time
- Unexpected events

Work Hacks for Time Management

To many working professionals I know, achieving work-life balance remains elusive and seems more like wishful thinking than a realistic goal. They never seem to have enough time to get work done even though they spend many hours at work and even take it home. With the availability of high-tech devices, they seem to be on call 24/7. As a result, they have less personal time and feel more stressed. They wonder how they can spend less time working and still get their work done in order to have more personal time. This is an essential life skill and habit. Much like fitness, this is a muscle set to build and develop. It will also get better with practice and regular conditioning, so it pays when you start this early in your career. Tight timelines and limited support resources are common situations in business. However, you can learn to manage effectively. I have seen many examples of individuals who outshone others because they had strong project management and resource management skills. From work-life balance perspective – the balance between devoting time to work and stopping to smell the roses along the journey – I learned to plan my time intentionally, mindfully and smartly.

POWERFUL WORK HACKS

In this chapter, I will look at non-productive and time-wasting activities we do at work, ideas to reduce these activities and a strategy to prioritize so we can focus on getting work done more effectively and efficiently.

TIME-WASTERS

According to a Harris Poll and CareerBuilder survey report on American workers (Economy, 2015), the top 10 time-wasters are:

1. Cell phone/texting

2. Gossip

3. Internet

4. Social media

5. Snack or smoke breaks

6. Noisy co-workers

7. Meetings

8. Email

9. Co-workers dropping by

10. Co-workers putting calls on speaker phone

WORK HACKS FOR TIME MANAGEMENT

I modified the above list from my observations and ranked them as follows:

1. Cell phone/texting/social media.

2. Gossip/socializing. This includes hallway mingles and long lunches.

3. Internet browsing on non-work activities.

4. Excessive number of meetings, including team meetings, project meetings, company/organization meetings, one-on-one meetings, emergency meetings, etc.

5. Email (reading and responding). This includes personal and work email.

6. Taking extra coffee/smoke breaks throughout the day.

7. Interruptions. This includes people coming by and interrupting you at your desk.

8. Commute time. This depends on where you live and how far you are from work. In many locations where traffic is terrible with no convenient public transportation, this can impact your time significantly.

While these findings were specific to American workers, I submit that they are not too different in your specific country. In addition to the above time-wasters, unexpected events, which may be out of your control, can consume a significant amount of your time.

For example, your manager comes to you with an urgent request or you get called into a meeting to clear up the confusion from a previous meeting. Furthermore, when you get sick and have to take time out of work, your work is not getting done and the longer you're out, the further behind you get.

According to *The Telegraph*, half of all workers waste up to two hours a day (Huth, 2015). I would say that's a low estimate. But even two hours is a huge amount of time that could have been used to get more work done. Imagine if you could cut that time in half and use that time to get your work done and be able to leave earlier, how much more productive your life would be.

HOW TO REDUCE UNPRODUCTIVE ACTIVITIES AND MANAGE TIME MORE EFFICIENTLY

It's unrealistic to eliminate all "non-work" activities. Moreover, it can be beneficial to our well-being and productivity to spend some time on those "time-wasting" activities. Taking a coffee break or a short walk helps us clear our mind. We cannot go through the whole day without touching base with our friends or responding to our family. Hallway chats are a good way to build relationships with our co-workers. The idea here is to not spend excessive amount of time on these activities but to keep them in moderation.

Here are the best practices to help you reduce time-wasters and be more productive:

WORK HACKS FOR TIME MANAGEMENT

- Reserve two continuous hours every workday to work on your highest priorities. If possible, choose the time when you do your best work – early morning, for example. Block this time on your work calendar to prevent people from scheduling meetings with you during that time. Otherwise, your calendar is an invitation for people to schedule you. Of course, there are times when you won't be able to keep this time for yourself, but be disciplined and try to stick to this practice as best you can.

- When you get an unexpected request from your manager, determine if you are the best person for this request. It tends to be by default that managers automatically come to the person they trust and depend on to get the job done. Refer to the "Work Hacks for Saying No" chapter to help you with this situation. One benefit of the two-hour block is that you have "extra" time to work on your manager's request in case you didn't have to use all of that time.

- Apply discipline to determine which meetings you need to attend versus the optional ones. Usually, we have many more meetings at work than necessary. Whenever there is an issue, someone will call a meeting instead of trying to see if it can be addressed offline by a few key people associated with the issue. And if there are meetings where you and a team member are invited and the purpose of the meeting is information-sharing, determine if you and your colleague can take turns attending. To help you decide whether you need to attend a meeting, ask yourself what the impact to you would be if you skipped it. Moreover, many meetings are run inefficiently, running longer than scheduled; worse still, multiple meetings are held to go over the same topic. While this sometimes is necessary, it's frequently a result of poor meeting management.

- If you and your team are preparing for an important presentation to company executives, you probably need to review your work with your manager and others before meeting the executives; this exercise can be time-consuming. While it's a good idea to have your manager's support before you present, there are ways for you to manage this task more efficiently.

- Unless you need to work at your desk, find a guest workstation or an empty conference room where you can hide and do your work. Since a majority of interruptions are not important, this reduces the potential disruptions from people coming to your desk unexpectedly. If an urgent matter comes up and you're not at your desk, people will either email you, call you on your cell phone or text you.

- Taking coffee breaks or walks is a good way to clear your mind, but be disciplined about the number of times a day you do this. Sometimes people come by your desk and invite you to take a coffee break; you can factor this into your daily number of breaks. Also limit the amount of time you spend on coffee breaks and be disciplined about it. However, we're not robots so we will need to be somewhat flexible with the times when we want to take more or longer breaks with our colleagues, but they should not be frequent occurrences.

- Moreover, resist spending time on the internet for personal use. If you need to, by all means. But before you start, ask yourself if you need to do it right now and what would be the impact if you did it later in your personal time. The risk of internet browsing is that once you start, you can move from one site to another or from one topic to another and lose track of time. Similarly with social media, unless you cannot wait, make a habit of using it during your break or lunch hour. Again, ask yourself the same question: what would happen if you waited to do it later in your personal time. In terms of texting, we do use it as a regular form of communication since it is quick and we can do it pretty much at anytime and anywhere. For non-work-related texting, limit yourself to when you take coffee breaks or your lunch hour. Let your friends or family members know you may take some time to reply to them.

- Emails are a notorious time-waster and they come in all forms – junk email, information-only email, personal email, work email that you need to reply to, etc. There could be hundreds of email arriving at your inbox daily. Use filter tools to filter out as many spam emails as possible. If you're unorganized with email, it can cost you a lot of time when you need to find a specific email urgently but have no idea where it is. One way to combat this is to organize your email folders in ways that work for you and help you locate email quickly. You can organize your email by main topics and have sub-folders for topics within the main topic folder. For example, you may have different "job" folders (folders containing materials you need for your work), one for each functional area you work with, and folders for external company partners you interact with. You may want to have a dedicated folder for email messages between your boss and you. This will help you quickly find a particular message and a good way to indirectly organize your boss.

• Moreover, prioritize your email by working on import-ant/urgent emails first and leave non-urgent or unimportant ones for later. Lastly, make a habit of cleaning up your inbox on a regular basis. Having hun-dreds or thousands of emails in your inbox is a recipe for trouble when you need to find a specific email.

• Similar to email, organizing your computer folders will help you reduce time trying to look for forgotten files. I have seen disorganized employees who put all their working files on the desktop screen regardless of the document type, and later on spent precious time trying to locate a file among a forest of files. This laziness wastes valuable time. A few minutes of setting up a folder structure would have saved them a great deal of time later on.

- Getting sick is something we don't really have control over. Unfortunately, when we get sick, we're out of commission and may quickly fall behind on our work. Our work doesn't go away when we're sick and will pile up waiting for us when we come back. However, what we can do is to keep ourselves healthy and fit as much as we can. When we're unfit and stressed out, we are more vulnerable to getting sick. Fitness experts and doctors agree that a 30-minute workout done three times a week is good for our body and mind and helps us be more productive. If you're away from work and falling behind due to illness, you may want to ask your boss for an extension or to assign your work to someone else if the deadline is important.

- Working at home from time to time helps reduce the commute time significantly, especially if you live far from your workplace. Even working at home during morning rush hours can save you a lot of time. Many companies allow work flexibility such as working at home some of the time. Check with your company and your manager to see if this option is available to you. At one point, I lived an hour away from work with no convenient public transportation and it took at least two hours of commute time each day. That was a huge amount of mostly unproductive time. However, I was able to work at home two days a week, which reduced my unproductive commute hours significantly.

HOW TO PRIORITIZE

We are inundated with many work activities and projects, from small to big tasks, from unimportant to urgent and important. We can get overwhelmed trying to figure out how to prioritize our work and deciding which things to tackle first. While there are many complex tools, high-tech applications and devices to help us prioritize, I believe simple tools and methods are often more effective. Below are a few practical methods to consider in prioritizing your work.

1. **Important versus Urgent** – popularly known as the Eisenhower Box (Brandall, 2016). Important tasks are defined as:

   ▷ People or projects are affected if the task is not completed.

   ▷ Other tasks depend on completion of this task.

   ▷ The task contributes significant value.

Urgent tasks are defined as:

   ▷ The task required to be completed is overdue or soon to be.

   ▷ The task demands immediate response and action.

   ▷ The consequences of not doing the task will be felt quickly.

You put your tasks in one of these boxes. If you have multiple tasks in the box, you prioritize the tasks within that box based on business needs (for example, does your manager's request have higher priority than your own task?)

Urgent and Important **Do it now**	Important but Not Urgent **Decide when to do it**
Urgent but Not Important **Delegate it**	Not important and Not Urgent **Skip it**

2. **Four category boxes** – a similar concept to the above method (Brandall, 2016).

Things you want to do and need to do **Do it now**	Things you want to do but do not need to do **Decide when to do it**
Things you don't want to do but need to do **Delegate it**	Things you do not want to do and do not need to do **Skip it**

3.My modified method – a variation of the first method that I use is as follows. I carry a work notebook where I take notes from meetings and write down information or things I learn throughout the day. I reserve a number of pages near the end of the notebook for me to list all the "To Do" tasks. Then I write the priority code and deadline for each task. For example:

▷ The task: Complete business metric report for Quarter 3

▷ Priority level: 2 (important but not urgent)

▷ Due date: July 10 (3 weeks from today's date)

On the notebook page, I write: "#2. Complete business metric report for Q3. July 10." I cross off each item from the list when I complete it or if I don't need to do it anymore. The advantage of this is I can keep a running list and add or cross off tasks as appropriate. It also allows me to keep a history of all the tasks and it gives me a sense of satisfaction when I cross a task off the list when completed. While there are a multitude of e-planners or calendars on phones or computers to keep track of this information digitally, I find that writing things down also helps me remember them. Instead of using a notebook, you can do the same thing using an Excel spreadsheet that allows you to sort on the priority code or timeline as you want.

WORK HACKS FOR TIME MANAGEMENT

In Asia, time management and prioritization are important management skills and are seen as an important factor in separating top-tier performers. Even as companies are flattening their organization structure, they are still selective with the higher levels. If you have a desire to move up the chain and be part of the management team at some point, the sooner you develop this skillset and get ahead of others early in your career, the higher your chances of breaking out from the crowd. Time management is also an extension of efficiently using your resources. Perception of being average in this area could delay potential advancements.

A few more suggestions to consider:

- Develop impatience on wasting time, especially those "fragmented slots" while waiting, on public transport or coffee time. Use those times for learning and thinking. Sum up those fragmented 10 minutes to be greater than the sum of all. I would purposefully block out time slots in my schedule to pack up the day's "add-on" agenda. It would discipline me to be more conscious on time management throughout the day and focus my time for those "add on" topics. Focusing on a topic for a continuous 30 minutes is much more effective than revisiting the subject in between meetings or breaks.

- Leverage the tools you have to manage your time. Outlook, Dynamics, Dingtalk or a simple To-do list are good handy tools.

- Practise eliminating and summarizing to focus on core value-add. That will help separate objectives and means-to-an-end and to focus our time on what matters. I often witnessed meetings and discussions going too long and with no concrete resolutions, especially in large meetings and with emotions running high. In those situations, I would ask to confirm the objectives of the meeting. I would then summarize what was agreed and eliminate what was not helping the objectives. That usually would refocus everyone's attention back to the meeting's objectives.

- Generate ideas while exercising. I found this to be very useful and productive. If it's not in your routine, please try. I have many of my marketing creative ideas and business breakthrough concepts from my runs or swimming laps.

I'm confident that if you follow the suggestions in this chapter, you will be able to get more done at work and reduce the work you need to take home and, as a result, have more personal time to do what you like.

Work Hacks for Dealing with Changes

It's a given that the only thing constant in the workplace is change. It was kind of a running joke in my company that we could expect a major re-org every year. During my career spanning over 25 years, I have worked in 12 different organizations in five companies. I worked under 12 managers and experienced numerous company organizational changes. I can tell you my companies were not the exception; most of the people I talked to and interviewed also confirmed this. It's highly unlikely you will have the same manager or work in the same organization, same company in your entire career. Some changes will be the result of your decisions while other changes will be out of your control. Company organizational changes can be unnerving and introduce uncertainties. Many people don't handle changes well and take a long time to adjust. However, if you're able to deal with changes effectively and adjust to the transition quickly, you will be able to not only maintain but also enhance your standing in the company. In this chapter I will discuss possible changes at work and how to deal with them while maintaining your relevance in the organization.

Changes At Work

- Impact on you? Yes
  - Your job
  - Your role or scope changed
  - Your team
  - Moved to a new team with new manager
  - Your manager
  - New manager replaced current
  - Your company
  - Company acquired or merged

- Impact? No/limited
  - Your colleagues laid off
  - –
  - Moved to another team, changed new manager
  - Company reorganization

While it's a given that changes in the workplace will happen during your career, the first crucial rule is to recognize what you can control and what you cannot. In Stephen Covey's book, *The 7 Habits of Highly Effective People*, he talks about the circle of concern and the circle of influence (Covey, 2002). Many of us focus on the concerns and react to things we can't control, rather than focus on areas we can influence and proactively work on. Covey encourages us to focus our energy and proactively work on things we have influence over, thereby expanding our circle of influence. For example, your manager decides to leave the company and you end up having a new manager. Instead of focusing on your concerns and fear about the new manager, you should focus your positive energy on what you can influence in this new situation, such as helping the new manager get up to speed quickly with the new team.

Regardless of any organizational change in your workplace, the key is to first focus your time and energy on the changes that you have some control or influence over. Secondly, do your best to behave and act professionally – stay calm, keep things in perspective, focus on your work and avoid getting emotional or distracted. Just the fact of recognizing you don't have control over a particular company change will help you avoid taking it personally and keeping you sane. Thirdly, make sure your own "house" is in order – meaning your annual plan is up to date with clear job responsibilities, specific goals, results you have achieved to date as well as expected deliverables for the remainder of the year. If you have not updated the plan, work on it as soon as possible because it's an important document to demonstrate your role in the organization.

Here are several common company changes and ways to handle them.

- **Company changes/reorganizations**. Your team/department is moved to another organization under a new executive. An example of this move: currently you are a pricing analyst on the pricing team in the Product Management organization. With the company reorganization, the team is moved to the Finance organization headed by a Vice President of Finance. In this company organizational change, we will cover two scenarios: one where you still work for the same manager and one where you have a new one.

  ▷ **You still have the same manager**. In this scenario, your manager's initial objectives are: (1) to establish her and her team's credibility by educating the new executive about her and her team's role and value to the company; and (2) establish a good rapport and working relationship with the new executive. At this point your manager should treat this transaction as a new beginning with her boss and to find out as much as she can on how to work with the new executive effectively. With your knowledge of your manager's style, strengths and weaknesses, you should take this opportunity to offer her help during this transition. Meet with your manager as soon as possible and ask her for specific tasks you can help. Keep in mind this change is new to your manager as well and she may be feeling a lot of stress and pressure to establish her place in the new organization.

For example, if your manager is disorganized and needs to prepare certain materials quickly for a meeting with her boss, she would welcome your help. Taking this initiative would further enhance your value to your manager.

▷ **You have a new manager**. In this scenario, the new organization's executive has chosen a new manager for your team. It's logical to assume the new manager already has a working relationship with her boss and may not know much about her new team's role and value to the company. Your objectives here are to educate your new manager about your and the team's role and value to the company as well as establish a good rapport and credibility with her. If the new manager has not already done so, seek a meeting with her. When you have the meeting, use the time to update her on the role and value the team offers. Review with her your annual plan and give your thoughts on business challenges and priorities. Although you're a member of the team, taking this initiative to discuss the team with her shows your leadership and your broad knowledge of not only your job but the overall picture of the team. In addition, ask your manager for any specific requests she may have that you can assist in this transition. Finally, take the opportunity to find out how to work with her going forward.

If your new manager comes from outside the company, she probably knows little about the company's business, organizational dynamics and about you and the team. There is a lot for this manager to get up to speed on; she may focus initially on syncing up with her boss, trying to understand the company business and as a result, may not put as much energy toward her team. Here, you have a great opportunity to make yourself valuable by proactively bringing her up to speed and sharing your insight on the team, the company and its challenges.

A friend of mine, Katie, recently went through this experience. Due to reorganization in the company, the Vice President of her group and his direct report were forced out (or "retired to spend more time with family") and Katie was worried about whether she would be next in line. The new VP, who came from a different industry, had little experience with the new company's business and industry. Katie seized the opportunity to work closely with the new VP. She helped bring her up to speed on the inner workings of the company business and she created presentation materials for the VP's important meeting with the company's executive staff. The VP was impressed with Katie's skills and deep knowledge about the company and its business. By taking this proactive approach, Katie established her credibility and positioned herself as a valuable asset to the VP.

Whether your manager is new to the company or not, after she has had time to digest the team information and meet her boss, you should ask to review your annual plan with her to see if it should be updated given the recent organizational change. New managers tend to want to add their own footprint to their organization and tend to make changes to their team and the team's charter. Your manager will appreciate your taking the initiative in helping her put her stamp on the team and succeed in the new role. By establishing your credibility and value, you stand a good chance to keep your job, or better yet, get a chance to be assigned to a more important role on the team. Lastly, you should proactively plan for the next step in your career; it's best to take control of your career and not put your fate in somebody else's hand or wait to see what happens next. By proactively exploring your options and planning your career, you're in control and have the confidence to drive your career.

- **You have a new manager replacing the previous one**. There's no change in company organizational structure. For situations where your new manager comes from outside the company or from another team, the discussion above applies here as well. The exception to the above situations is that this is less complicated since the organization structure remains the same. If you have been in this organization for any extended time, you should have a good understanding of the company's business, organization dynamics and priorities. As a result, you are in a great position to help the new manager get up to speed and to influence her on the team's priorities and needs.

If the new manager is one of your peers who was promoted, it may present a bit of an awkward situation and resentment among the team members, especially if you and other members feel the promotion was not warranted. However, once the decision is made, you have no control whether that person is your manager or not. While it may be difficult, you need to do your best to be professional and not let your personal feelings influence your behaviour. If you find this promotion completely unacceptable, you have a choice to explore different job options. If you choose to stay in your current position, at least for the time being, you must try your best to have a good professional relationship with the new manager and help her be successful in her new job. Keep in mind the new rookie manager is probably feeling a bit insecure as well and would appreciate your professionalism and best effort in working with her, although some new managers in this situation react to their insecurity by being more hands-on. As difficult as it may be, maintaining your professionalism by focusing on your work will gain the respect of your new manager and people in the company. Lastly, never burn bridges. It's a small world and things tend to have a way to come back to you.

- **You move to another team and have a new manager**. In this situation, you should already have some familiarity with the new manager, whether you wanted to move to that team or were assigned to it, and that should make establishing a rapport with the new manager easier. However, you should proceed as you would in other new management situations and work with the new manager to find out how best to work with her. In addition, since you're joining a new team, use the initial time to get to know the team – how they work together, their concerns, how they work with other teams and how you can best work with them.

- **Your colleagues get laid off but you are not affected**. While this situation doesn't impact your employment status with the company, it will likely have an effect on you. In the short term, you may feel sad and sympathetic for your friends, disappointed or upset at the company's decision even while you feel relieved you still have your job. It can also be a difficult time for your manager. I have had to give the bad news to employees who were impacted and it was one of the least favourite parts of being a manager. I experienced a mix of emotions – sadness to lose an employee/friend, guilt of affecting someone's livelihood, failure that I wasn't able to keep this employee. One of the things you can do during this time is to be as low-maintenance to your manager as possible. In the near to medium term, the layoff may have a real impact on the manager and the team's workload, particularly if no replacement resource is available to cover the gap left by the laid-off employees. If this happens, the manager needs to prioritize and figure out how to cover the workload gap. This is where you can help your manager and yourself.

Help your manager prioritize the workload, and at the same time, influence her to allow you to take on more value-add work and take some of the less important work off your plate.

- **Another team gets a new manager**. While this may seem to have little or no impact on you or your team, it actually can. Much of your work involves other teams and when a team inherits a new manager, that manager may change her team's priorities and the way they work with you and your team members. As a result, it would be good for your manager to hear from the new manager about any change in priorities and how both teams can best work together. Don't assume that things will continue to work as usual. Remember, new managers tend to want to put their own signature on the new team they inherit. So talk to your manager to find out if your manager has met or plans to meet with the new manager. If not, explain to your manager the importance of syncing up with the new manager to avoid future miscommunications or disconnects which can derail the project both teams have been working together on. You can say: "Have you had a chance to meet with the new manager? This project is important to both teams and it would be helpful to us to get her thoughts so we can be on the same page." Your manager understands that potential project mistakes would not reflect well on her and the new manager and would appreciate your taking the initiative.

- **Your company gets acquired or your company acquires another company**. This can be a nervous time for employees in both companies, especially if there are overlapping functions, product lines and services. This raises the likelihood of the company cutting cost and laying off people. As the companies begin the integration process and if your team is potentially at risk, your manager would likely be involved. The best you can do here is to control your own "house". Make sure your annual plan is up to date and your manager is clear about your role, responsibilities and contributions. Make sure you stay in contact and maintain a good relationship with your network contacts. They can help you explore opportunities.

When my company merged with a competitor, it was clear there were overlapping products lines. Our business unit (BU) had similar products. Once my company announced that our BU products would be replaced by the other company's products, we all knew we'd be soon out of a job. Since I had maintained a good relationship with my network contacts, I was able to meet with several of them to explore job openings and opportunities in their organizations. Through these contacts I was able to land a position I liked.

Work changes are stressful and at times affect you subconsciously. Don't underestimate the impact and be aware if your temperament changes abnormally. Don't bring stress from work home as it is very unfair and damaging to family health. Check it at the door. Recognizing the stress early and talking with your family would greatly help you and improve your state of mind. If possible, get ahead of the change by volunteering to join the transition project team. This gives you advance notice of impending changes. I was involved in a few re-organizations and in Programme Management Office (PMO) to plan out the organizational changes. From my experience, it's much better to be involved early and plan forward. It allows more time to adjust to a new world.

Take a proactive approach to personal change management. Adjusting your mindset to the big picture quickly enables you to think through organization directions and plan out your next steps. Companies are not able to plan for each employee. Also, Asian markets tend to be at the downstream design process of the worldwide planning cycle. While you may not know what's coming, preparing yourself to accept potential changes will enable you to use your energy and time to plan the best path forward.

Work Hacks for Business Communication

You may have heard of the expression "When in Rome, do as the Romans do". Whether you work for a multinational company with headquarters in the United States or for a local/national company who works frequently with other companies, customers, partners, suppliers and others in the US or other Western companies, you should apply that motto in your daily work life interacting with your co-workers, managers/executives, customers, partners, etc. Business culture is a way of business operations and it defines how employees at different levels communicate and act with one another and with others outside the company. Understanding American or Western business culture, knowing how to conduct yourself and how to use business idioms is essential to your success. This chapter will show you how.

Understand and Use Business Idioms

Increase communication effectiveness

Else lost in conversation

Else could lose opportunity to be heard

Be seen as part of the team

Speaking "tribe" language

Do you understand that phrase?

Yes → **Add to "language bank"**

No

Read list in chapter

Assimilation of learning

Ask ← *Common practice for your colleagues to explain to you*

WORK HACKS FOR BUSINESS COMMUNICATION

AMERICAN BUSINESS CULTURE

America is a big country with more than 300 million people in 50 states. As a result, regions can differ from other regions on the culture and even one company can have some cultural differences from other companies. However, there are common themes, and while this may seem simplistic, I believe two phrases define American business culture:

1. "Results/Goal-Oriented"

2. "Time Is Money"

These two themes explain how Americans conduct business at work and how they interact and work with one another to get things done.

1. **Results/Goal-Oriented.** When employees start out on a new project, their focus is on achieving the project's goal. Forming personal bonds with team members is not a top priority. Now, if in the course of working and achieving results, they develop close bond with certain team members, that's wonderful. But they don't go into a business transaction with the focus of forming a strong bond with their counter parts. As a result, they tend to take individual initiatives and heroic acts. Americans also have a more favourable view on aggressiveness (or some would prefer to call it assertiveness). I'm not making judgment one way or the other, just pointing out certain unique characteristics of American business culture.

2.Time Is Money. With respect to time, being on time is expected, especially if there's a business meeting with clients or partner companies. Americans strive to get things done with just the right amount of time needed, with no unnecessary wasted time. They sacrifice other things in order to spend time working. My European counterparts commented on American professionals' strange practice of eating lunch at their desk. There are even "working lunch" meetings, unheard of in a lot of countries. But as much as Americans hate wasting time, here is a paradox: they sit through endless number of meetings. Sometime there's a meeting to talk about what was decided in a previous meeting. You know what one of the most common complaints from Americans is? Yes, too many meetings at work. I remember the times where I sat through meetings all day and ended up doing work in the evening at home. Oftentimes I think people attend meetings because they're afraid they may miss something important if they don't go.

Now that we have covered the two phrases defining American business culture, let's look at some key characteristics to give us deeper insight to the culture, and more importantly, prepare us to thrive in this business culture.

AMERICAN BUSINESS CULTURE CHARACTERISTICS

- **Yes means yes.** By and large, Americans are direct and speak their mind, especially in business environments. If they don't agree with you or have a different viewpoint, they speak up and voice their opinions. This is particularly important on matters requiring decisions or active discussions that may impact them. If someone disagrees but doesn't speak up, it is taken as agreeing or at least, not opposing. This can be quite a surprise and a bit of a shock for someone from a different culture where avoiding conflicts and avoiding embarrassing others in public is a good social practice.

I had my first lesson when I initially worked with my co-worker in Japan. As a team lead, I needed to have the team members agree with the project assignments and so I assigned certain tasks to my Japanese co-worker. Being immersed in American business culture, I took his silence as acceptance since I assumed he would've spoken up if he didn't like what I proposed. A couple of weeks later when we had our team meeting to go over the project's status, he didn't show any progress. When I emailed him afterward, he replied that he didn't agree to take on the assignments. An element of Japanese culture is being polite and a desire to please people. Saying no is uncomfortable. So instead of objecting, my colleague remained silent. From that incident on, I learned to confirm or clarify with him to avoid any misunderstanding.

One note of clarification: as I mentioned above, not all regions in US are the same in terms of culture. In regions/areas where there's a lot of diversity, with people from different backgrounds and cultures working together, the American culture has somewhat evolved and taken on a balanced blend of traditional American business culture and other cultures. For example, people are still direct but in a more diplomatic and friendly way. However, this requires you to be able to be more aware, to clarify and read between the lines to understand what they really mean. In my experience, I find it most effective in the workplace to employ a direct approach – a way of being direct while showing your understanding and without offending the other person. This is the approach I try to demonstrate throughout this book.

- **Greeting characteristics.** In general, Americans are personable, friendly and expressive. While some other cultures discourage making eye contact or shaking hands, as it's seen as disrespectful, American business culture is just the opposite, where making eye contact, looking someone in the eye while talking, handshaking and smiling are widely practised. Another characteristic is informality. Americans refer to each other by their first name in conversations in casual and even business settings. They don't often use titles, even with their superiors, unless it's appropriate and needed for the occasion.

Upon meeting someone for the first time or being introduced, Americans proactively look at the other person's face, smile, say hi and their name, and extend their hand to shake the other person's hand. And if there's time, they then engage in small talk as a way to break the ice and build a rapport. If this social greeting practice is unfamiliar or uncomfortable to you, realize that it is normal practice in America, not disrespectful, but an excellent way to start a business relationship and get off on the right foot. Practise it with people you are comfortable with and it'll be more natural to you after a short time.

One more note: "How are you?" is a very common phrase Americans use to greet one another. However, it is not an invitation to divulge our medical history (especially with someone new). A simple "Fine, thank you, and you?" is sufficient.

- **American business language: Idioms.** One important element of business culture is the way people use business language to communicate or express themselves – known as business idioms. They often are "shortcut" communication phrases people use so they don't have to spend more time explaining what they mean. Understanding the commonly used business idioms and knowing how to use them yourself will enable you to communicate more effectively with different audiences and impress them with your business language skills.

Imagine a scenario where you're in a meeting and people are using a lot of business idioms unfamiliar to you. You would be lost in the conversation and not able to contribute meaningfully. And you also lose an opportunity to be heard and recognized by other people in the meeting. Communication is required to be an effective team player. Learning business idioms is like learning a local language and it is a most effective way to be accepted as a member of the team.

In the following pages, I describe the common business idioms in American business environments and provide examples on how they are used. There may be other idioms not included here, or new ones created in the future. Don't worry. Many people, even people who have lived and worked in US for many years, don't know or understand all the idioms. When you hear a business idiom you don't understand, ask that person to explain it to you. This is a common practice and they will be happy to oblige.

WORK HACKS FOR BUSINESS COMMUNICATION

Idiom	Meaning	Example
24 by 7	24 hours a day, 7 days a week.	"I'm working 24 by 7 these days."
A chip on your shoulder	Someone holding a negative feeling such as feeling disrespected or resentment of being overlooked.	"Sometimes he behaves in the meeting like he has a chip on his shoulder."
A tough break	Something unfortunate or unlucky happens.	"It was a tough break for our manager when her best employee left the company."
Ahead of the curve	To be more advanced than other people or companies.	"We're #1 in our market because we're doing our best to stay ahead of the curve."
Ahead of the pack	To be better or more successful than the competition.	"If we want to stay ahead of the pack, we're going to have to continue to innovate."
ASAP	"As soon as possible."	"I need to leave the meeting now. My manager wants to see me ASAP."
At stake or a lot riding on the line	A significant outcome or result is at risk.	"There's a lot at stake with this project."
At the end of the day	What you consider is the most important or relevant thing about a situation.	"At the end of the day, I'm the one being held accountable for my decision."
Back to the drawing board or back to square one	To start something over and go back to the beginning.	"The product demo didn't work. We have to go back to square one."
Ballpark number or figure	A rough estimate or forecast.	"My ballpark figure for sales this month is 5,000 units."

Idiom	Meaning	Example
Beat a dead horse	Discussing or talking about the same issue over and over.	"Haven't we beaten this dead horse enough?"
Behind someone's back	To do something to someone or relating to someone without that person's knowledge and in secret way.	"You went behind my back to talk to my manager without telling me."
Behind the scenes	Something or event that happens in secret or not in front of the public or people.	"The marketing event went smoothly because the team did a lot of work behind the scenes."
Behind the 8-ball	A difficult position from which it is unlikely one can escape.	"I don't know how I can get this project completed on schedule and under budget. I'm really behind the eight-ball."
Between a rock and a hard place	A situation where one is faced with two equally difficult alternatives.	"You're between a rock and a hard place. I don't envy your decision."
Big picture	Looking at a higher, strategic goal or outcome instead of the details.	"Although you are busy with a lot of the details, don't lose sight of the big picture of this project."
Bottom line	Summary or conclusion of a discussion or an issue.	"The bottom line is we can't afford to pay for this marketing event."
By the book	To do things according to company policy, rules or procedure.	"He doesn't want to take any risk so he does things by the book."
Catch someone off guard	To surprise someone by doing something that they were not expecting.	"I was caught off guard when my manager asked me to travel on a business trip for him."
Cave (or cave in)	To agree to something that you or someone did not want to accept previously.	"The salesperson finally caves in to the customer's demand."

WORK HACKS FOR BUSINESS COMMUNICATION

Idiom	Meaning	Example
Come up short	To try to achieve something but fail to get the desired result.	"The promotion was supposed to generate 10% increase in sales, but we came up short."
Cop out	Using an excuse to not do something.	"That's a cop out for not wanting to take on the action item."
Corner a market	To dominate a particular market.	"Microsoft has cornered the PC market with their Windows OS."
Cut corners	To take shortcuts and find an easier or cheaper way to do something.	"They cut corners in order to get their product to market sooner."
Cut one's losses	To stop doing something that is not meeting the end goal even though some amount of investment had been spent.	"Our marketing campaign was expensive and not showing results, so we had to cut our losses."
Cut-throat	Something that is very intense, aggressive, and merciless.	"The PC market is a cut-throat industry."
Cut to the chase	Tell someone to get to what they really want to say and not ramble or beat around the bushes.	"I don't have a lot of time to listen, can you cut to the chase?"
Diamond in the rough	Something or someone that has great potential but will require a lot of work.	"He is a diamond in the rough. He's smart with many great ideas, but he doesn't know how to work with people."
Drop the ball	Someone or some persons failed to complete a task that they owned.	"We didn't complete the project on time because you dropped the ball."
Fall through the cracks	Something needed to be done but no one was aware or took initiative to do it.	"The computer needs to be fixed but no one did. It fell through the cracks."

POWERFUL WORK HACKS

Idiom	Meaning	Example
Fifty-fifty	Something is divided equally – 50% for one person, 50% for the other, or something that has an equal chance to succeed or fail.	"We have a 50/50 chance of completing this project on schedule."
From the ground up	Starting or building a business, project, or something else from zero.	"Steve Jobs built Apple company from the ground up."
Game plan	A strategy or plan.	"What is your game plan to compete against your main competitor?"
Get back in/into the swing of things	To get used to doing something again after having a break from that activity.	"After a long layoff, I'm trying to get back into the swing of things."
Get the ball rolling	To start or resume something such as a project.	"Our project deadline is coming soon. We need to get the ball rolling now."
Get or be on a person's good side	If someone likes you, you are on their "good side".	"I have a new manager and I want to be on her good side."
Get a foot in the door	To take a low-level position with a company with the goal of eventually getting a better position.	"I like this company a lot so I just want to get my foot in the door first."
Give someone a pat on the back	To tell someone that they did a good job.	"The VP gave me a pat on the back for giving a good presentation to the customer."
Give the thumbs up (opposite is thumbs down)	To give approval or endorsement.	"We're excited because management gave our new proposal the thumbs up."
Go for broke	Willing to risk everything to achieve a desired result.	"I went for broke to win a big customer deal."

WORK HACKS FOR BUSINESS COMMUNICATION

Idiom	Meaning	Example
Go down the drain	When someone wastes or loses something.	"He spent a lot of money on an expensive computer that didn't work. All his money went down the drain."
Go the extra mile or the extra step	To do more than what was expected in a positive way.	"He went the extra mile to make sure the product demo would work perfectly."
Go through the roof	Results are increasingly exceeding expectations.	"Our sales are going through the roof."
Ground-breaking	Something is new and innovative.	"The iPhone was a ground-breaking piece of technology when it was launched.'
Six of one, half a dozen of the other	The alternatives are the same.	"You can choose to work on challenging project A or difficult project B. It's six of one, half a dozen of the other."
Hands are tied	A person who does not have control over a situation.	"I would love to help you out, but my hands are tied."
Have work cut out	A person has a lot of work to do or a particularly difficult assignment or tight deadline.	"We have to finish our design in 2 months. We have our work cut out for us."
Hit the nail on the head	To do or say something 100% correctly.	"You hit the nail on the head. That's exactly correct."
Hold your horses	To slow down, to thoroughly think through a situation before making a decision or moving ahead.	"Hold your horses, I'm still trying to follow what you're saying."

Idiom	Meaning	Example
In a bind	You're in a tough situation where any decision you make or action you choose has some undesirable results or trade-offs.	"I'm really in a bind. If I decide to help you with your project, I have to say no to my other important project."
In a nutshell	In a few words.	"In a nutshell, this book is about succeeding at work."
In the black (opposite is in the red)	If a company is "in the black", the company is making a profit.	"After losing money last quarter, our company finally is in the black this quarter."
In the driver's seat	To be in control.	"We've achieved 90% of sales target with 3 more months to go. We're in the driver's seat."
Jump the gun	Making a decision or statement too early or quickly before the right time	"Jim jumped the gun by accusing my software as not working when he hasn't even looked at his software yet."
Jump through hoops	Do everything possible to achieve a goal or please someone.	"I have to jump through hoops to get my proposal approved."
Keep me in the loop or keep me posted	Telling someone to continue to inform you of their status or progress of a situation.	"Keep me posted on your job interview."
Keep one's eye on the ball	To give something full attention and to not lose focus.	"To reduce the number of software bugs, we need to stay focused and keep our eye on the ball."
Get up to speed	To learn something new in a job or a project and to become knowledgeable.	"I joined the company one month ago and I'm getting up to speed."

WORK HACKS FOR BUSINESS COMMUNICATION

Idiom	Meaning	Example
Long shot	Something that has a very low probability of happening.	"Getting a promotion this time is a long shot for me, but I'm going for it anyway."
Lose ground (opposite: gain ground)	To lose some type of an advantage (market share, time to market) to a competitor.	"Our company gained ground on our competitors in market share this year."
More than one way to skin the cat	There are different ways or solutions to a problem.	"That's one solution to this problem, but I think there's more than one way to skin the cat."
No brainer	The decision is really obvious or really easy to make.	"Joining this company is a no brainer. They gave me more pay and better job position."
No strings attached	Something is given or offered without expecting anything in return.	"We offer our customers the use of our products for 6 months with no strings attached."
Not going to fly	An idea, proposal or solution that's not going to work or get approval.	"I don't think your idea is going to fly with our manager."
Off the top of one's head	Giving a response without thinking about it much or doing any research on the subject.	"I'm not sure how many customers we have, but off the top of my head, I'd say about 200."
On a roll	Continuing successes.	"We beat sales quota the last 3 quarters. We're on a roll."
On the ball	To be alert, aware and get things done.	"My new team member is really on the ball. He's really doing a good job."
On the same page	Two or more people are in agreement. about something.	"Let's go over the contract terms to make sure we're on the same page."

POWERFUL WORK HACKS

Idiom	Meaning	Example
On top of something	To be in control of a situation and aware of changes.	"I try to stay on top of the latest market changes in my industry."
On your toes	To be alert.	"Stay on your toes. Anything can happen in this uncertain market."
Out of the loop (opposite: in the loop)	To not know something that a select group of people knows.	"I felt like I was out of the loop after taking time off from work for the past couple of weeks."
Out on a limb	To make a statement, suggestion or assumption that is risky and bold.	"I'm going to go out on a limb and predict that we will finish our project under budget."
Play hardball	To be very aggressively competitive and to do anything possible to win or get what you want.	"He's a tough negotiator who plays hardball working on a deal."
Play it by ear	To wait and see what happens before moving on or taking the next step.	"Before we change our pricing, let's play it by ear and see what happens in the market."
Put all one's eggs in one basket	To put all your resources and trust and rely on only one thing to bring success.	"You should apply to many different companies instead of just one. Don't put all your eggs in one basket."
Put the cart before the horse	To do or think about things in the wrong order.	"They were trying to get management approval on a proposal before completing their business plan. They were putting the cart before the horse."
Raise the bar	To set the standards or expectations higher.	"We raised the bar in our industry with our latest product innovation."

WORK HACKS FOR BUSINESS COMMUNICATION

Idiom	Meaning	Example
Read between the lines	To understand something that isn't communicated directly, to understand what someone is implying or suggesting.	"In reading between the lines, I think our manager will approve this project."
Rock the boat	To cause problems or disrupt a situation.	"Not sure if I should ask to be transferred to another project. I don't want to rock the boat."
Round-the-clock	24 hours a day.	"I'm working round the clock today."
Run around in circles	To do the same thing over and over again without getting any results.	"We keep discussing the same issue in the last few meetings without making any progress. We're just running around in circles."
Same boat	If people are in the same situation, they are in the "same boat".	"A lot of people are worried about layoffs. Everyone's in the same boat."
See eye to eye	To agree with someone's view.	"We work well together. We see many things eye to eye."
See something through	To do something until it is finished.	"I want to see this project through before taking vacation."
Sever ties	To end a relationship.	"We had to sever ties with several of our suppliers due to bad materials."
Shoot something down	To "shoot something down" means to reject something, such as a proposal or idea.	"I try not to shoot down people's ideas during a brainstorming meeting. The goal is to generate ideas, not to judge them."
Shoot the breeze	Talk casually about non-work topic.	"We're just shooting the breeze waiting for the meeting to begin."

POWERFUL WORK HACKS

Idiom	Meaning	Example
Sky's the limit	There is no limit to what can be achieved.	"With this untapped market, sky's the limit on how much sales we can get."
Slam dunk or hit it out of the park	Very certain about a successful outcome.	"I think you hit it out of the park in your customer presentation today."
Smooth/clear sailing	A situation where success is achieved without difficulties.	"Once we fixed the major product glitch, it was smooth sailing to get product to market."
Stab someone in the back	When someone betrays another person's trust to pursue or advance their own personal agenda or position.	"He helped her get the job here. How could she stab him in the back by getting him fired?"
Start off on the right foot (opposite is "start off on the wrong foot")	To start something in a positive way.	"I want to start off on the right foot when I start my job with this company."
State of the art	Something that is modern and technologically advanced.	"We have a state-of-the-art research facility."
Take the bull by the horns	To take charge, especially on a difficult situation.	"Our project was going in different directions, so I had to step in and take the bull by the horns."
Talk someone into something (opposite is "talk someone out of)	To convince someone to do something.	"I was apprehensive to take on a new project I didn't know much about, but my manager talked me into it."
The elephant in the room	An obvious problem or controversial issue that no one wants to talk about.	"We all know our manager is the problem to getting things done, but no one wants to talk about this elephant in the room."

WORK HACKS FOR BUSINESS COMMUNICATION

Idiom	Meaning	Example
Think outside the box	To think of creative, unconventional solutions instead of common ones.	"With social media, we had to think out of the box on ways to promote our products."
Throw in the towel	To quit.	"After repeatedly being unable to sell my ideas to my manager, I threw in the towel."
Touch base	To make contact with someone.	"I'll touch base with you later today after I get out of my next meeting."
Twist someone's arm	To persuade or convince someone to do something that they don't want to do.	"I had to twist his arm a few times to get him to agree to our proposal."
Up in the air	Something is undecided.	"With the new management team, things are up in the air."
Uphill battle	Something that is difficult to achieve because of obstacles and difficulties.	"Trying to convince his customer to leave our competitor and join us will be an uphill battle."
Upper hand	Someone has an advantage over someone else.	"Our main supplier has a key product we need that we can't get from someone else. They have the upper hand in pricing negotiations."
Water under the bridge	Past history which is being forgotten, forgiven, or no longer to be emphasized.	"We had a work problem in our last company, but that's water under the bridge now that we've joined a different company."
Win-win situation (opposite is "lose-lose")	A "win-win situation" is a situation where everyone involved gains something.	"We negotiated a contract that both parties are happy with. It was a win-win."

POWERFUL WORK HACKS

Idiom	Meaning	Example
Word of mouth	People hear about something through informal conversation with friends, family members, acquaintances, etc.	"One of the best advertisements is through good word of mouth."
Writing on the wall	Evidence and clues that something (usually negative) is going to happen.	"He's going to get fired. The writing is on the wall."
Yes man	A "yes man" is someone who always agrees with their superiors.	"The marketing manager just wants to hire yes men."

Work Hacks for Office Politics

Workplace or office "politics" means the use of influence, power and social networking within an organization to achieve goals or changes that benefit the organization or the individuals within it. Many of us view it as a dirty word, even immoral. We view the people engaging in work politics as selfish, dishonest people who play dirty tricks, backstab, suck up to the right people and do whatever they need to do to get what they want, regardless of what damage they cause. We don't want to get anywhere near these people. If you are one of the people who view politics this way, I would like to present a different view, one based on my professional experience and that of many people I've worked with.

Politics exists in any company and organization. Politics is about human interactions and relationships, and as long as there are people interacting and working together, politics is a part of life. It's not the office or buildings that create political behaviour, it's people. While many of us associate political skills or behaviour as undesirable, it's up to us to practise good politics or bad politics. For sure we have seen undeserved people who got promoted

Handle Politics Smartly

Effective strategy

Identify powerful people, via:
- Organization chart
- Informal network

Get mentor to champion you

Understand decision process

Find common ground

Seek strategic focus

Mindful of threats

Pick your battle

Build your case

Know your "enemy"

Maintain professionalism

Basic skills

People/teamwork

Credibility

Goodwill

Expertise

Visibility

by using their political skills, by scheming their way and by sucking up to the bosses. However, from my professional experience and talking to many executives, high-performing and successful employees are skilful politicians who practise good politics with the right intention – striving to achieve win-win outcomes, influencing people in a positive way and thinking "team first". People who achieve some success through practising bad politics by backstabbing, spreading false rumours, bullying with "me first" attitude eventually will be exposed and they won't be able to sustain their success in the long term. Be confident that you can definitely participate in workplace politics without compromising your value or integrity. Especially in American business and corporate environments, having good political skill is crucial to your being able to get your work done, and to achieve great results and success throughout your career. This skill is a must in business culture all over the world. It took me a long time to realize a mindset change is essential to look at smart politics as a necessary tool. My direct manager Jos once told me that I'm politically savvy. I was surprised, did not like it and definitely didn't read that positively. But he clarified that I'm politically aware but just not very participative. I like to reiterate the point that good politics is part of your survival tool kit.

In this chapter, I'll describe what skills and qualities are required to be good at workplace politics, and I'll show effective strategies to "play" office politics.

SKILLS AND CRITERIA TO BE EFFECTIVE AT WORKPLACE POLITICS

- **People/teamwork skills**. As I mentioned earlier in this chapter, politics is about human interaction and relationships. While you don't have to be best friends, you must be able to work well with people. These fundamentals include communicating, collaborating and negotiating skills (conflict resolution included). Having patience and really listening to people is a key part of being a good communicator. All good communicators are good listeners. Your colleagues will appreciate you when you go out of your way to help them when they need it. This will also earn you a lot of goodwill that will come in handy when you need it later. Being able to resolve issues and conflict in a professional manner without getting personal will endear you to them and earn their respect. I cannot emphasize this skillset enough.

- **Credibility**. Building credibility is something you earn over time. Credibility is earned by meeting our commitments, delivering excellent results on time, being dependable, and helping out when needed. This applies to everyone you work with, including your team members, colleagues, managers and executives. You need to do this continuously. Keep in mind that while it takes continuous track records to build credibility, you can lose credibility quickly. So remember to continue maintaining and building your credibility and not slipping up on your commitments.

- **Trust and loyalty.** You can earn trust and loyalty by being a good team player, by putting the team ahead of yourself and by showing genuine care for your co-workers. People will more likely give you the benefit of the doubt because they believe you are honest and you put the interest of the team ahead of your own. Respect what people say and genuinely seek to understand instead of being condescending and talking down to them. People in turn will reciprocate their respect to you and their trust in you. When you speak up, people will listen, take your words at face value and not have to wonder if you have any hidden agenda.

- **Goodwill credit**. You can accrue goodwill credit that you can use when you need help getting your idea through the corporate political process in the future. You can achieve this by helping your boss and other people succeed and making them look good. I once had a manager who said my most important responsibility is to help him succeed. If your boss is respected and has credibility with their peers and bosses, they can be your strong advocate in helping you sell your ideas. And by helping other people succeed, they know you put the team's success first and would be more than willing to support and carry your idea forward. I covered this in detail in the chapters on "Work Hacks for Promoting Yourself" and "Work Hacks for Managing Up".

- **Expertise in a key area**. Being viewed as an expert in a key area expands your sphere of influence. You are seen as a "go to" person. Important people in the company and executives rely on you for your opinions and recommendations. A person could be an expert in a new and emerging technology, a master presenter or a business analyst guru while someone else could be recognized as a creative marketing expert. When I was in Product Operations, we had a person who was responsible for Business Analytics and Metrics. She was the person our manager and other executives went to when they needed a thorough analysis on a business problem, or company reports to prepare them for upcoming meetings with industry analysts. Everyone knew her as the go-to person in the business analytics area. Having "power" or "influence" is a key element to succeed in playing office politics.

- **Visibility**. If people don't know you, you will have a very difficult time persuading people in the company to buy into your idea. If you are recognized and are viewed positively by important people in the workplace – your manager, other managers, executives, influencers, key decision-makers, etc. – they are much more likely to meet with you and listen to your ideas and opinions. Getting an opportunity to meet with them to sell your idea is half the battle. You must seek out opportunities to get visibility with key people in the company.

EFFECTIVE STRATEGIES FOR WORKPLACE POLITICS

Now, let's look at practical strategies to navigate workplace politics (Mindtools, 2019).

- **Identify powerful people**. Since politics is about people using their influence and connections to achieve their goal, knowing who the powerful people are is obviously one critical element to your success in workplace politics. From my experience, it is important for you to read the big picture. Go where the ball is heading. If you can see what you boss or higher management wants or where they are going, you should align towards that intent and be part of the actions. That helps you to be part of the strategic focus or key initiative.

  ▷ Study the organization chart. Begin at the top with the CEO and the Executive staff. Obviously the buck stops with the CEO. However, CEOs don't normally make every decision. It's not possible even if they wanted to since they need to focus on the strategy and direction for the company, and they would rather focus their limited time on the most important and strategic decisions.

  While most important decisions are discussed and made at CEO/Executive staff meetings, one or more executives are responsible for driving the details in the meetings. For other decisions, certain executives decide or have their own management staff drive the decisions. In addition to the CEO/ Executive staff organization chart, look for the organization chart of each of the executives on the CEO's staff. It shows you what department they lead and gives you an idea of the type of decisions they are driving. Moreover, you'll see the executive's management staff and that will give you more breakdowns of their department and respective reporting management staff. Depending on the size of the company, the number of management layers can vary, from very flat one or two management layers to six or more. In the most recent company I was at, there were seven layers – from the individual contributors to the CEO.

Refer to the figure that follows for an example of an organization chart of a Fortune 500 company. The CEO organization chart should be on the company's website. The other organization charts (for example, WW Marketing Exec/Staff chart, or the middle management chart for the Product Marketing group) can be found on their respective internal company websites. If not, contact their administrative assistants for the most recently updated charts. Since management turnovers are not unusual, make sure you keep up-to-date organization charts.

▷ In addition to the decision-makers you can identify fairly easily on organization charts, key influential players and gate-keepers are just as important for

WORK HACKS FOR OFFICE POLITICS

you to acquaint yourself with. These people may
not have executive titles nor can they be identified
by their titles. Executives and decision-makers
oftentimes value their opinions and rely on them for
relevant information to help them make decisions.
They are sometimes view as the right-hand people
of the executives. Executive Chief of Staff and Executive Administrative Assistants oftentimes are key
gatekeepers. They control access to executives, set
and manage executive agendas, and determine the
information flow to them. While they may not be
involved with the content of the decision, they are
no less important in determining your effectiveness
and success in navigating workplace politics. I was
Chief of Staff for a Senior VP in the Product Operations organization of a Fortune 500 company for a
year. I set up his meeting agendas, determined for
the most part the issues to be discussed, reviewed
people's requests to meet with him one-on-one,
and decided what information to provide him. So
you can see that while I wasn't making decisions, I
had a great deal of influence at managing workplace
politics in his business unit.

▷ Find informal networks. These networks are not
  shown on the organization charts. They comprise
  employees who share some common ground – such
  as team members on a company initiative, members working on key strategic plans, members of
  company social clubs, participating members of
  company sporting events or company-wide events.

131

These people tend to share some interests, knowledge or passion in a particular area; they meet regularly or periodically, sometimes outside of work hours, including lunch breaks or after-work social hours. Since company management and executives are aware of many of these networks, they pay attention to them, give them a lot of visibility, and lean on them for insight and viewpoints. As a result, these networks can have significant influence on the decision-makers.

▷ Find out about these networks, pick one or more that are of interest and benefit to you and find ways to join them. Talking to your co-workers, managers and mentor is a good way to identify these informal networks. Company newsletters or communications oftentimes include news and updates about these groups and their activities as well as invitations for people to join them. Pay attention in meetings or presentations to see who has visibility and credibility with executives. Through these tactics, you'll be able to identify not only these networks, but also who the leaders are. It's always easier to join these networks if they already know about you and have a good impression of you. So it'll benefit you to continue to build credibility and trust in your workplace. Refer to the "Work Hacks for Promoting Yourself" chapter for more information.

- **Get a mentor who can be your champion**. A mentor can do wonders for you. A well-respected and connected mentor has a lot of insights you can tap into that you can't get easily. They know the key decision-makers, influencers, important informal networks, and they know how to get things done effectively. Not only are they fantastic resources for you to test your ideas and seek advice, but they can also help you sell your ideas and get buy-in from key decision-makers and influencers. While I didn't think much of it early in my career, I became convinced and appreciated having a mentor. When I first met with my mentor, I had very little idea of organizational politics and how to work with different people to get work done. Over a long period of time having regular one-on-one meetings with him, sitting in executive meetings he participated in, meeting key people he introduced me to and whose networks he helped me join, I truly understood and appreciated how to play workplace politics and I am truly grateful to him to this day. To identify potential mentor, observe in executive meetings, watch speakers at company wide meetings or presentations, ask your manager and talk to your colleagues. Ideally, your mentor should be at least at your manager's level or even above and also someone who is well liked, well respected and valued by people in the company. Once you know who you would like to have for a mentor, ask your manager to help you or if that mentor knows you and has a good impression of you, ask them yourself.

- **Understand the decision-making process**. A key element of understanding the decision-making process is knowing who the ultimate decision-makers are so you have good insights on how to develop your game plan. Depending on the size of the company, different types of decisions may be made by different people. In a medium/large company, decision-making is delegated to the appropriate people. For example, a decision of allocating resources to an engineering project may be made by the Head of Engineering or an Engineering Department manager, while a decision on whether to cut an important project is decided by the CEO/Executive. A decision on going ahead with a marketing event may be made by the Marketing PR (Public Relations) manager, while a decision to form a key strategic marketing alliance with another company is decided by the Marketing Executive. More narrow and specific decisions may be made by middle or lower-level managers or even team leaders, such as whether to do additional testing or what equipment to use for a customer demo event. At small companies, most decisions – whether big or small – may be decided by the CEO and a couple of executives.

Understanding how decisions are made is another important element. Are they made by consensus with a group of people or by one leader with input and recommendation from the working group and others? Are the decisions top-down or decided collaboratively? If you are a group leader working on a project and the decisions are made by consensus, you know you need to get buy-in from all the key participants. If the decision is ultimately yours with input from others, you can structure your meetings and discussion accordingly. Similarly, if you or your team needs approval on a proposal and the decision is made collaboratively by a group of managers, including your boss and their peers, then you know you need to get buy-in from all those participating managers. Obviously, the more consensus the decision-making process needs, the more challenging it will be, and this is where you'll earn your pay with your political skills.

So how do you go about understanding the decision-making process. You'll be able to develop a good insight by talking to your manager, your colleagues, picking your mentor's brain, asking to sit in to observe key decision-making meetings at all levels – CEO meetings, department head meetings, team meetings and project review meetings. When I left a company to join another company as a Pricing Strategist, I learned from my previous experience. I requested my manager (and he agreed) to take me to his meeting with the Executive Staff. He introduced me to them and described to them my role. After sitting in the back of the room and observing several sessions, I gained a good insight on the inter-workings of the group – whom did people listen to, who asked the right questions, who was the master at working the room, who was seen as the leader/decision-maker. I also learned about the decision-making process – it was very much collaborative and discussions could be lengthy with many differing points of view. I also did the same with other lower-level meetings.

- **Find common ground**. Common ground helps people gravitate towards each other and gives them a rallying point to work together. Find out what people are interested in, what they are passionate about, what their goals are, and similarities you have with them. In order to get people to gravitate toward you and to be excited working together, you first must establish your worthiness to them and to the company. You can accomplish this by exhibiting the skills and qualities I described in the first section of this chapter. Once people experience and see this first-hand, they will trust you and you will have gone a long way to be effective at managing workplace politics.

With the example I mentioned above when I joined a company as a Pricing Strategist, I learned from sitting in meetings and talking to different people that the Senior Executive VP of Strategic Planning, who was widely respected, has a serious passion for pricing. During any meeting where pricing was discussed, she would perk up and engage even more than normal in the discussion. Recognizing this, I asked for a one-on-one meeting with her where we discussed in-depth about the company's pricing challenges and I got a great insight into her thinking. After the meeting, she asked me to set up monthly meetings with her to go over and discuss all things pricing. You can imagine my excitement about this opportunity to get such an important person to be an advocate for me. So keep your ears and eyes open and look for common ground.

- **Pick your battle and build your case**. Part of knowing how to play politics in the workplace is knowing when to fold, when to go for it and how to go for it.

  ▷ Pick your battle. Throughout your career, you'll have many opportunities to take on, to lead and to shepherd projects through the organization. Not all opportunities are equally important or strategic, and while some opportunities are attractive to you, they may not be to your manager or company executives. It's important to show strong conviction, but realize that some opportunities you think are important and beneficial to your company, your manager and/or other managers may not share the same belief.

  Although your idea maybe a great idea, it may not be a priority for the company. The first rule is to ensure the idea you want to pursue is aligned with key decision-makers. When working in product management for a mid-size company in the early 2000s, I had a colleague, David, who believed strongly the company must develop a blade storage server soon. Without convincing data, he nevertheless persistently pushed his case to the VP of Product Management and even after the VP made it clear that while the idea had potential, the market was not ready for this technology and the company had other more urgent priorities to pursue, David would not let it go. He became obsessed with his idea and grew increasingly frustrated, causing a lot of tension between him and the VP and between him and the engineering team. Out of frustration, he quit the company and did not leave on good terms. While one can argue for the validity of his idea, David did not make sure that his idea aligned with the key decision-makers' priorities, let his ego get in the way and did not pick his battle. I think it would have been better for David to put his idea on hold, work on another opportunity that aligned with the company's priorities and continue to gather research and go back to his idea at a better time in the future.

▷ Build your case with strong supporting data, credible intuition and stay with your conviction. Many executives, especially today, are driven by data and analytics. To be successful in getting buy-in for your ideas, you must prove your ideas have merit and facts. "Flying by the seat of your pants" or "swinging from the hip" proposals will likely not see the light of day. With the increasingly intense competition and the need to continue growing in sales and profit, companies must be selective in picking which opportunities to pursue. While intuition based on experience is important in considering potential ideas, it's not sufficient for decision-makers. Combining intuition and analytics and showing your conviction will give you the best chance of getting their approval.

When I managed a team of senior professionals at Hewlett-Packard, I hired a consultant, Robert, to research on a potential server opportunity. After extensive research, Robert was convinced that the company needed to develop a server technology to allow data centre customers to rack many servers in a tight space. I scheduled a review meeting for him to present his case to the General Manager's executive staff. At this meeting, he presented a compelling case on the need to develop this technology due to financial implications and competitive threats, and to bring it to market soon. However, two key executives did not agree with his recommendation. They were conservative and did not want to take the risk of spending millions of dollars on this prospect, even though the potential financial returns would be significant. After a lot of going-around-the-circle discussion, the executives still did not want to make a decision. Robert stood firm in his conviction, saying: "I'm not saying we need to do this for my own satisfaction. You hired me to do this work so you can reject my recommendation and I'll go on to the next project, but I strongly believe we must do this for the reasons I've discussed." Everyone was a bit stunned hearing this, but I think they were impressed with his conviction and that he was making his case for the right reason. That he was willing to put his job on the line showed his strong conviction. The difference between Robert and David from the earlier example is that while both had strong conviction, Robert showed he was willing to walk away as much as he didn't want to, and David stuck to his idea to the bitter end.

▷ Get frequent feedback and address issues right away. With the Robert example above, one thing I would have done differently would be to have Robert meet individually with the executive staff to learn about their concerns so he would be better prepared to address them in the meeting.

- **Seek out opponents and strive to understand them**. Most of us have a tendency to stay away from and ignore people who oppose us, oppose our ideas and who just want to shoot down our ideas. However, this would be the wrong action to take. You probably have heard the saying "Keep your friends close and your enemies closer." You want to not only know who they are but also why they oppose you or your ideas so you can take counter or preventive actions. Moreover, they may have legitimate reasons or concerns about your idea and if you know why, you can find ways to address them and come up with a win-win solution.

When faced with this situation, you should meet with them with an open mind. You can establish an open dialogue by telling them about your objective, letting them know that you would like to hear from them and get their feedback, and committing to them that you would address their concerns. The key word here is "listen". No need to get defensive; stay with the subject matter and don't get personal. If they get personal and attack you personally, do not let them. Let them know that you want to focus on the business issue and want to get their feedback, not personal insults or comments that are irrelevant to the idea. Ask for specific feedback and examples, not general comments. That should reset them to focusing their comments on the issue. If that doesn't work, thank them for their time and let them know you're always open to their input. At least this way you know whom you can work with and whom you can't.

- **Maintain professionalism**. I've heard often through-out my career that "So-and-so is such a professional." People view these professionals with respect. These people focus on building relationships, working with people to solve problems, thinking out of the box to find creative and win-win solutions. They focus on the business issues, not personal issues. They seem calm, maintain their poise under difficult situations and don't get ruffled. Moreover, they tend to be optimists – glass-half-full people who don't waste their time with rumours. When things are not going their way or when they are facing setbacks, they don't whine or complain. Instead, they focus on not just bringing problems to management, but bringing potential solutions as well.

Of course, we are all humans with a full range of emotions. However, knowing how to express and control ourselves is important to play the political game. We have seen many real politicians who lost their elections because of one outburst. I have seen co-workers who lost their cool and started lashing out at their managers and other managers in meetings. They later regretted it but the damage was already done. Their outbursts painted them as immature people who don't have what it takes to function well under pressure. These people ended up receiving poor performance reviews and eventually leaving the company. If they did not learn from their experience when they moved on to another company, I think they'll likely repeat the same mistakes and face similar consequences.

If there's one advice I have it is this: The way to keep your cool and stay under control is to not take what people say or criticize personally. Focus on the business issue and even when other people get personal, you stay laser-focused on the issue and push them to get back on track with the issue.

Work Hacks for Making Small Talk

In today's social media world, face-to-face conversation skills are being diminished and not used as much. But make no mistake, being able to conduct conversation is as an important part as ever of our work and career success. While texting and chatting online has a convenient role in our daily life, it is not a common method of communication at a social outing or work event where people meet and conduct small talk with one another. Take an example: when you attend a business meeting with your co-workers or customers and before everyone begins serious discussion about the meeting topic, people engage in casual small talk to break the ice, to put people at ease and to get comfortable with one another. It sets the mood for a productive meeting. If while people are engaging in small talk you're sitting or standing alone by yourself and not part of the small talk, you would feel left out and somewhat awkward. It would make you less a part of the meeting when the discussion begins.

So what is small talk? It is a short, friendly conversation about a common topic. Small talk can take place among friends, co-workers, between executives and employees or strangers. It takes

Engage in Small Talk Naturally

Preparation

- Be well-informed and prepared
- Be proactive
- Remember and address people by name

Approach

- Really listen
- Identify common ground
- Engage with positive energy
- Body language
- Begin with ice-breaker
- Discuss safe/fun general-interest topics

Exit

- End conversation thoughtfully
- Set up follow-up discussion if needed

Avoid

- Religion and politics
- Offensive jokes
- Personal wealth
- Embarrassing family issues

place in all kinds of situations: business meetings, interviewing for a job, making a presentation to customers, company business social outings, industry conferences and seminars, etc. It is an important people skill. The ability to make small talk in business settings is important because it allows people to be friendly at work without getting too personal. It also helps us build and expand our networks and helps us do our job more effectively.

If English is not your native language, you may feel uncomfortable talking to people in business settings or related social events. But even many native English-speaking people have the same apprehension. Many or most of us are apprehensive about these settings and are not comfortable going into a place where we don't know the people there and don't really want to spend time talking to them. However, remember that it is an important skill and will benefit you and your career. Moreover, it's not hard to learn and doesn't take long to be able to do it well.

No matter if you are an introvert or extrovert, you need to prepare this necessary business skill in social etiquette. You should not equate business small talk to unpleasant tasks but think of them as relationship-building and information-collection events. For international engagement, there are some customs to be aware off, especially what not to do. You should also learn some interesting things about the people you're meeting and use that knowledge to show that you care and have genuine interest in them. It is easier than you imagine. For example, I was visiting Korea on business during the World Cup soccer tournament. Everyone in Korea was into it. So, I researched on the Korean team's performance, colour of uniform, tiger crest and the Red Devils fans. The next moment I was watching the game with the

Korean business team and customers, drinking soju. I was definitely part of the team.

In this chapter, I'll discuss the strategies as well as specific ways for you to master and conduct small talk like a pro (Napier-Fitzpatrick).

- **Focus on the other person**. Having a curiosity and interest to learn about people will naturally help you put your focus on the other person when you talk to them. People are much more engaged and drawn to you when they sense that you genuinely want to get to know them. If you feel self-conscious talking about yourself, focusing on the other person will make you more comfortable and less self-conscious. Let me share with you a little secret: most people like to talk about themselves – it makes them feel good and important. It's a great way to establish a good connection and build rapport. I shared an example of this earlier in the book. Chloe, a friend of mine, told me about a dinner meeting with a client. Through the entire dinner, she made a conscious effort to focus her attention on her client. She asked a few open-ended questions and spent the rest of the time listening. When they said goodbye after the dinner, her client thanked her for an enjoyable evening and commended her for being a great conversationalist, even though for most of the dinner, Chloe just sat back and listened. We'll go over some techniques for engaging in small talk later, but I hope you can see that it's easy to make friends, to leave a great impression by focusing your attention on the person you're talking to.

- **Really listen**. Sometimes we listen but we may not hear what other people are saying. The highest compliment you can pay to another person when talking to them is to really listen to them, to make a real effort to understand what they're saying. Through listening, you show your focus is on them and that you are fully engaged and genuinely interested in them. One excellent way to show your listening ability is by asking open-ended questions, listening to their comments and asking additional questions and/or offering your own comments. Starting your question with "how/why/what" encourages them to explain and give more details, which in turn allows you to ask relevant follow-up questions. Although this is a two-way conversation, the fact is you just need to ask a few questions and the other person will do most of the talking, willingly. You'll be popular and make easy friends this way. You may wonder if people would be "turned off" if they think you're asking too many questions. While this is something you'll need to keep in mind, my experience is that we tend not to ask enough questions. So the risk here is low.

- **Identify common ground.** This can be a common topic that both you and the other person are interested in, a hobby you both share, a common issue you both are dealing with, an event that you both had recently attended or are interested in going, etc. Once you find common ground, whether with a co-worker, your boss/executive, business customer, or someone you haven't met before, you'll be able to communicate easily and naturally. At a recent social function with my co-workers and their respective spouses and significant others, my wife, Ann, was seated next to a co-worker's wife, Julie. Although my wife and Julie had never met, I noticed my wife and Julie were engaged in a lively conversation and they seemed to focus on one another. During a break, I told Ann that she and Julie seemed to have really con-nected. She shared that after exchanging hellos and polite pleasantries, they discovered a lot of common ground. Their kids had grown up and were soon to go to college, and they were interested in some mean-ingful hobbies they could do part-time. Ann shared with Julie a business hobby she has started and they were talking about what potential business hobbies Julie had the skills for and might be interested in exploring. They decided to hook up in the future to continue their discussion.

- **Be well-informed and prepared**. Stay up to date with world, work and local current events and news through watching or listening to TV/radio shows, reading newspapers, magazines and online sites. This helps you prepared to engage in small talk about a potential wide range of topics and gives you the flexibility to talk to more people, depending on their topic of interest. I spend a little bit of time everyday to learn about the latest news and what's going on in the world, at my company, in my city, not only to keep me up to date but also because I'm genuinely interested in knowing. In America, sport is a big interest, from team sports such as football, baseball and basketball to individual sports including tennis and golf. Travel and entertainment are also popular interests, including popular destinations, music, concerts, movies and theatre plays. Investing a little bit of your time keeping up to date in these areas will boost your confidence and make you comfortable engaging in small talk.

- **Be proactive**. Don't wait for people to come to you to say hello and talk to you. This makes you look apprehensive and not confident. If you are a bit shy or introverted and don't feel comfortable being there, know that there are likely many other people who feel the same way. So think of this as a chance to push yourself beyond your comfort zone. You are prepared, you know how to engage in small talk and convince yourself that this is a chance to show your small talk skills. So take the initiative and initiate the contact. Be the first to say hi and introduce yourself. If you had met someone before but don't remember their name, introduce yourself again and try to remember their name. I find saying their name in the course of your conversation makes it more personal and makes the other person feel good that you remember their name. This shows your confidence as well as your interest in meeting them. They'll come away with a good impression of you.

- **Engage people with your positive energy and body language**. Friendly eye contact and a warm smile show your interest to meet and talk. Maintain eye contact when listening and talking to them. Open your arms and use friendly hand gestures. All these are great ways to show your energy and enthusiasm of being there and mingling with people. Of course, remember to be genuine and don't overdo it. Things to avoid include looking at your watch or checking your phone too much while engaging in small talk. Or worse, texting your friends while talking to someone. This happens more often than not and shows a lack of courtesy and respect for the other person. I have seen too frequently at business meetings, company functions or social outings where people are constantly focusing on their phone with texting or engaging in online conversations while in the company of others. This does not create a good impression and it's best to be aware of and avoid this habit.

- **Begin the greeting with an icebreaker.** An icebreaker is a general statement or question to open a way to meet new people and also helps to jump-start conversations. For example, giving a compliment, asking about the event details, the location, how the person is associated with the event, even about the weather, are good ways to start a conversation. If the other person is from your company, ask what department they're in and what they do. If both of you are from the same department, ask about some news or event both of you have heard or attended recently. For example, "What do you think about the marketing training event last week?" or "Tell me about the technology networking conference last month" are good icebreakers after saying hi and introducing yourself. Remember to use open-ended questions to get people to talk more.

- **Discuss general-interest subjects.** When you have an opportunity to engage in small talk, remember to find a good, fun and non-controversial topic. This shows you are an approachable and friendly person to talk to. Some of the more common topics you can use for small talk include sports, music/movies/books, travel, hobbies, food/restaurants, jobs/occupations, technology, money/finance (housing cost, investments, etc.) and family-related topics (children, education, etc.). These topics are safe, not too controversial and mostly about sharing information and experience. And even if someone offered different views on a topic, people wouldn't get offended or strongly object. For example, when I talk to my co-workers about movies we've seen recently, we comment on what movies we saw and what we liked or didn't like about it. Even if we feel differently about the ending of the movie, that's okay and doesn't cause any issue between us. In business settings, even discussing a general topic can lead to unexpected opportunities. This was how I got my start in teaching at a well-known university. At one particular social function, I met and started a conversation with a friend of a co-worker's about the state of education in the US and the lack of professors with professional experience. I then told him that that's why I was interested in teaching in the future. It turned out that he was teaching at a university. A few months later, he contacted me and introduced me to the Dean of the Business School and I got my first teaching gig.

However, one word of caution when talking about family/personal matter: depending on how well you know the other person, use your judgment on how much personal information to share or how deep you want to ask about their family or personal situation. This may not be appropriate in business settings.

Here are some phrases you can use to start small talk and keep it going:

▷ Have you seen/heard...?

▷ What did you think of...?

▷ How did you find out...?

▷ Have you ever been to...?

▷ What is your favourite/least favourite...?

▷ Who is your favourite/least favourite...?

▷ What is your experience with...?

▷ What do you recommend on...?

- **Exit thoughtfully.** In many business situations, it may be important to make contact with many people in the place. The challenge occurs when you have limited time for small talk and need to find a good way to end the conversation and move on. Find an appropriate point in the conversation to make an exit, such as when the other person has just finished a thought or concluded a story. You can say: "It was great meeting and talking with you. I look forward to meeting you again in the future." If there's a business opportunity or matter you want to discuss, ask for their business card or tentatively schedule a time you'll contact them.

SMALL TALK MISTAKES TO AVOID

When you make small talk, try to avoid topics that are personally sensitive, or may upset the other person. Some topics to avoid include:

- **Religion and politics.** These topics can be very personal, emotional and controversial if people disagree.

- **Family/relationship status.** It's okay to ask about someone's family, but only if you already know them and have a good idea they're okay talking about it. The general rule is to avoid painful or embarrassing family issues, such as divorce, death and marital/children issues.

- **Money/wealth.** Telling other people how much money you make or asking them how much money they make is inappropriate and should be avoided. This is especially sensitive in American culture.

- **Offensive jokes.** Avoid telling offensive jokes that involve racism, sexism, violence, and other inappropriate workplace topics.

Hopefully I have impressed on you the important role small talk has in determining your effectiveness and success at work. By being able to learn the art of small talk, you'll be able to gain more confidence, expand your people network and obtain useful insight and information. And finally, I hope you are convinced that it's not hard to develop ability to conduct and engage in small talk by learning the practical strategies and practising proven small talk techniques.

About the Authors

Dennis Mark has more than 30 years of experience in the Information Technology industry, holding senior leadership positions including Vice President and General Manager of Solutions & Services for HP Inc Asia Pacific. In his international consulting capacity, he provides business subject matter expertise supporting organisational development, critical research and business decisions.

Michael Dam is an Adjunct Lecturer at Santa Clara University, California. He conducts career talks at universities as well as teaching career workshops, and provides individual coaching to career professionals. Michael holds an MBA and participated in the prestigious Accelerated Executive Leadership Program at Stanford University.

Dennis Mark and Michael Dam's 2022 publication, *Thriving At Work: What School Doesn't Teach You*, was lauded as "an absolute gem" and "a must-have career 101 handbook".